Self Improvement

Self Improvement

Rudolf Allers, M.D.,Ph.D.
Former Professor of Psychology
Catholic University of America

Roman Catholic Books
A Division of Catholic Media Apostolate
Distribution Center: Post Office Box 2286, Fort Collins, CO 80522

Nihil Obstat: Arthur J. Scanlon, S.T.D., Censor Librorum
Imprimatur: Stephen J. Donahue, Administrator of New York, NY, January 23, 1939

ISBN 0-912141-65-4

PREFACE

THIS book deals with the difficulties man encounters in life insofar as these difficulties have their origin in human personality; it aims at showing that much more of the difficulties and troubles man has to wrestle with spring from his own personality, or even are of his own doing, than is generally believed. It deals with the many reasons why a man may feel dissatisfied with himself and may desire to become different. And it endeavors to show that this desire is not at all hopeless, that man has many more chances of changing and of making himself change than common opinion will concede.

The arguments of the following pages are drawn from experience. They are not mere ideas derived from some philosophical or speculative idea on human personality. But they are, nevertheless, based on a definite philosophy. No treatise on human nature, or any side of it, can indeed dispense with such a philosophical basis, nor does it ever, though some authors may not be aware of their starting from a definite and general philosophy. Many of the differences of opinion which give rise to such a lot of controversies in psychology and pedagogy —not to mention other fields of research—arise not because one scholar has got hold of facts the other ignores, but from their starting from opposite platforms, that is from their adhering to opposite philosophies.

This book is based on Christian philosophy and Christian morals. They supply the general trend of the reasonings, but they are not the point from which these reasonings start. All that is explained in the following chapters is based on experience. It is facts and not speculation. And these facts may, in a way, contribute to prove the general and philosophical point of view to be true and, therefore, to be the one which will be most helpful in arranging our life.

Its being based on Christian philosophy does not make this book a treatise on religion, nor even a religious book in the true sense of the word. Though the introduction of certain notions belonging to theology—e.g., of grace or Providence or sin—cannot be avoided altogether, this book is one of psychology and written from the point of view peculiar to the psychologist. Nor is it philosophical, though it is based on a definite philosophy and, sometimes, makes appeal to philosophical ideas. This book is, in the main, one of practice. Its intention is to make clear things every man may understand and to give advice every man may follow and to show ways accessible to everyone. One need not study philosophy to become better.

Nor does its being based on Christian morals make this book one on morality. It is argued indeed that the way prescribed by morals is not only the best, but also the surest, if we want to attain satisfaction and a life as free from friction as is allowed to man. This does not mean, however, that this book is on morals. So far as the statements of morals come in, they do so because they have been found by experience to be useful rules of human behavior.

A reader desiring to know more of the principles of the philosophy of human nature will be disappointed. The book is not on them nor on the theory of psychology. It is the outcome of many years of observation, of practice, and of intercourse with many people. It does not aspire at being more than a summary of these experiences. In summarizing these experiences many details had to be left out; a complete treatise on the difficulties of human life and of the mistakes made by man and on the reasons why these mistakes are made, would have to be much larger—if such a task can be done at all. The author is fully conscious of the incompleteness of his arguments. But he is also convinced of the fact that the mistakes, or faults, or bad habits, or troubles occurring in every man's life are, all of them, essentially of the same nature, and that it is, therefore, sufficient to describe and to analyze some few to help in understanding them all.

Many a reader will feel, when perusing these pages, that he has been told nothing he did not know already. And he will be quite right. All the things detailed in this book are, more or less, known to everyone; but they are known in a dim and veiled manner. They have to be drawn into the clear light of consciousness for the sake of becoming helpful. The writer of these pages hopes not for more than for just this: that his words will be found to state but things known; if they are known to everyone, they will be true and they will tell but some essentials of human nature. Truths have to be told and considered, and not only to be felt. As long as these truths are not made fully conscious, as long as they are not made the very rules guiding our life, they are rather useless. This book desires nothing more than to show to everyone that he knows already what is amiss with him and that he knows the ways how to improve. By putting these things openly before the eyes of its readers, this book hopes to enable them to use what they know and to do what they can.

We may know perfectly what things are contained in a dark room, and we may know also how to handle those things. But we do not see them really, nor are we able to use them until the shutters are opened and the light of the day is flooding in. To open the windows of the human soul is all this book can hope to achieve.

RUDOLF ALLERS.

WASHINGTON, D. C.,
Catholic University
of America.

CONTENTS

PART 1

ON THE NEED AND THE CHANCES OF IMPROVEMENT

1. Need We Change?

Need we change at all? Is it really necessary to become different or better? May we not go on being what we are and behaving as we do? We are not perfect, we are surely no saints. But as for being a saint, who can be expected to be one? They are exceptions—wonderful, admirable exceptions; but we, you and you and I, we were not born to be exceptions, and so, why worry about not being perfect? Surely our neighbors have many reasons, good ones and bad ones, for finding fault with us, and we are quite right in thinking in the same way of them. What they think of us we do not know exactly; but we can imagine it pretty well. Not being perfect, we cannot avoid giving offence sometimes and to some people. But we manage to get along with them quite nicely, at least as a rule, and there is no plausible reason why we should bother about changing or becoming better.

There are, however, some rather disturbing facts. One day a friend, or maybe someone we are but slightly acquainted with, will remark on our behaving wrongly on a certain occasion; or he will, because he is merely cross or because some words of ours have made him angry, suddenly reveal to us that he thoroughly disapproves of certain features of our character. We may get angry too, and oftener than not such a scene means the end of a friendship or, at least, a definite estrange-

1

ment. We feel sure that he is, of course, wrong; his words have evidently been dictated by bad temper; he never really understood us; we are quite disappointed at his behaving in such a manner; we are sorry to lose him, but after all, it is perhaps better to get rid of him, since he proved to be so little capable of understanding us. So we think, and we try to push back the things he said into some remote corner of our mind; but they will go on rankling, and they will, in some quiet hour, turn up again and give rise to an uneasy feeling as to whether he has not been right after all.

We may also become, without such an impulse from without, suddenly conscious of something being amiss with us. The accustomed feeling of being all right according to generally accepted standards, gives way to a definitely uncomfortable state of mind, a state of dismay, of disapproval, of—well, of bad conscience. We feel troubled in our conscience, not because of this or that single action—everybody has behaved rather badly sometimes in his life—but because of a feeling of not being what we ought to be, in a more general way; we feel ashamed of the single more or less bad actions we know; we repent them perhaps. They are surely painful to remember, but this pain is, so to say, localized and circumscribed, concerned with well-defined points of our past life, definite days, definite places, involving certain persons, and so on. But this feeling of uneasiness is different; it is a general discomfiture and dissatisfaction, pervading our whole being, more troublesome than painful memories are, because of its vagueness, of its not referring to some particular fact; it is a feeling as if everything were wrong with us and as if our whole personality were in need of a thorough cleaning and rebuilding.

There is probably no one not having felt, one time or another, such things, though there are quite a few

who are very clever in forgetting quickly these unpleasant experiences; at least they will not be noticed
until they turn up the next time.

There are other reasons too which may make us wish
for some change of our personality, even though we are
not too much dissatisfied with it. A man may, indeed,
conceive the idea that he would get along with his fellows much better if he were different; he may discover
that many of the troubles he encounters in his married
life depend on the way he takes things and on how he
reacts to certain situations; he may come to think that
his being not as well-liked as he would wish to be may
depend on himself and not exclusively on other people.
Disagreeable though this thought is, he has to face it;
he has to consider the possibility of his own deficiencies
and faults being at the bottom of his difficulties. The
very moment this idea comes to him, he cannot but ask
himself what is wrong with him and what he can do to
improve things.

There is, furthermore, the fact of what is commonly
called bad habit. This name covers things of a widely
different nature, ranging from some oddities of behavior, which are so far rather unimportant, to real immorality. Some "bad habits" are morally more or less
indifferent—an absolute indifference in regard to morals
does not exist—but nevertheless not to be neglected, because they become a nuisance to others and, often
enough, a serious handicap to the person addicted to
them. Needless to mention instances: the figure of the
man who is always clearing his throat, or of the other
who incessantly turns a pencil between his fingers; of
the woman who every second minute opens and closes
her bag with a loud snap; of the girl who cannot refrain from munching candy during a concert and
rustles the paper; of the person incapable of staying
quiet and who steadily fidgets, and of the representa-

tives of many equally unpleasant types sufficiently well-known.

Bad habits like these make a person appear rather repulsive. If a man has some remarkable qualities, people will put up with his disagreeable habits, though they will feel them to be as disagreeable as ever. They say of him: "He is very clever indeed, very instructed, rather interesting, quite nice, but. . . ." And there will always be some people with whom the "but" carries more weight than the rest of the qualities, be they ever so excellent. Harmless as such a habit may appear to the one who has it—if he is aware of it at all—it may become a very serious obstacle to success.

Some habits one would not just call immoral, are nevertheless a definite part of personality, and they may influence the relations with other people in a marked manner. To be a bad loser in play or in sport is not necessarily a sign of moral inferiority, though it may denote such a deficiency. The general suspicion aroused by such behavior is indeed not quite unfounded, though one has to beware of hasty conclusions. The habit of fair play in sport is, on the other hand, no guarantee of thoroughgoing morality; a man may quite well be absolutely fair in sports and very unscrupulous in business. Being a bad loser, however, or unfair in play gives rise to a definitely unfavorable presumption and becomes thus the reason of a good many difficulties in social life.

There are finally habits which are simply immoral. A person may be a habitual liar; he knows that by indulging in this habit he is not only breaking the commandments of ethics but also that he gets himself in trouble. He has had this experience quite a lot of times; he knows that he is sure to be found out; he really would prefer to be sincere and honest, partly because of the immorality of the thing and partly because of the inconveniences arising therefrom. He wants to become better, but he does not know how to begin. It is very cheap advice telling him that he simply ought to speak the truth henceforth and not tell lies any more. The trouble is that he will drift into his old habit without noticing it and without wanting to do so. Before he has time to reflect, he will give a false answer. And then, he thinks, it is too late; he must stick to his words and carry on his lie as long as it will last. His lying does not do any good, either to him or to others; he does not tell lies because he hopes to profit by them; he tells them because it has become a habit with him. And he would gladly get rid of this habit; he feels that he ought to change, and he would do so, if only he knew how to tackle this habit.

Some people are given to quite unreasonable fits of anger; others instead of flaring off in anger, become cross; both habits spoil the life of these persons and become a perfect nuisance to others. Certain persons are subjected to quite unreasonable attacks of fear; they discover enemies everywhere and feel surrounded by dangers threatening themselves or their relatives. Taking offence easily, feeling neglected, misunderstood, not loved enough, and what not, is also a rather frequent feature of behavior which does anything but further happiness.

These qualities are said to spring from temperament, and temperament is believed to be an inborn feature of personality and to be, accordingly, immutable, beyond the grasp of will; people having such an "unhappy temperament" would be very glad if they could behave differently; they are, however, convinced that nothing can be done.

Pages and pages could be filled by a list of reasons why a man wants to be different. But there is a far greater problem which has to be solved in the interest of society and of the general moral standard. This problem arises from the fact that there are many people whose character and behavior deserves a strict censure and who, nevertheless, are quite unduly satisfied with themselves and ignore altogether their having many, sometimes very grave, defects.

Human nature is subjected to many self-deceptions. But if we want to know whether we are on the right way, we have first of all to get a true idea of what we are. We may be wrong in being satisfied with our personality, but we may be equally wrong in holding the opposite opinion. The desire for change, for developing another character, assuming another behavior is not always the outcome of a sincere wish for moral improvement, not even always of a longing for greater efficiency; it not so seldom springs simply from vanity.

Knowledge of one's own self is said to be the first step on the way to improvement; we have to know who and what we are first, before finding out whether and in what sense we ought to improve. The most important thing, therefore, is to get a precise idea of one's own self.

2. *Can We Change?*

Though all the following chapters will demonstrate that we can change, and how far personality and character may change and that this change can be brought about by our own doing, it seems nevertheless advisable to make some few preliminary remarks on this subject. They appear to be indicated because there is a rather general conviction that character and personality are essentially immutable. The knowledge of being in need of change becomes neutralized and rendered ineffective by such a conviction. The prejudice of the immutability of personality may become a strong objection against all that will be detailed in this book. This prejudice cannot, it is true, be upheld any more after all the facts upon which the arguments of these pages repose have become known; but a prejudice may create a certain attitude of mind making it impenetrable, more or less so, even for very convincing reasons. It is, therefore, better to say right here some words on this topic.

People will readily agree that a man may behave differently, that he may change his behavior even so far as to make others believe in a radical change of his personality; but such a change is considered, generally, as a kind of fake, as playing a rôle or wearing a mask. A man may learn to behave in such a way as not to shock his neighbors; he may learn to adopt the customs of his environment and to behave as the other people do; but it is doubtful, so this very common opinion runs, whether he may ever really become different, that is, whether his being can change.

Many people are agreed, on the other hand, that a thorough change of behavior is to be expected only from a change of being. A behavior a person adopts because it is useful or agreeable to his fellows and because not adopting it would give rise to many inconveniences, cannot be upheld continuously; the "true nature" of such a person is sure to leak out sooner or later. Men who are able to carry through such a rôle during a lifetime and who are never found out, seem to exist only in fiction but not in reality.

A man wanting to become different finds himself, as it seems, in the dilemma of having either to play a rôle and to risk being found out or to give up becoming different altogether. The first does not appeal to a somehow upright mind, because it comes dangerously near to lying, even if there were not the risk of being unmasked. The second means going on suffering all the unpleasantness arising from one's present personality.

But this conviction of character being immutable is not so general as it is believed to be. Even persons who openly profess this opinion do not act according to it; if a man were indeed fully convinced of the immutability of character or personality, he never would try to influence other people and to make them different; but mankind believes, and did always believe, in education. Education means, of course, more than merely imparting knowledge and teaching a certain kind of behavior; it is also, and even mainly, formation of character. There are indeed some who declare that there is in truth no such thing as education; that man is essentially uneducable and that the only thing we can do is to train him in a certain way and teach him to refrain from actions which become disadvantageous to society and, therefore, have painful consequences for the individual. But even these people behave, when they have to educate others, as if they held quite the opposite view. Notwithstanding the professed unbelief in the power of educational influence, the general attitude proves that the opposite conviction is too deeply rooted in human nature to be destroyed by such pessimistic ideas.

Contrary to what some advocates of "progress" pretend, there is always some truth in the old and general convictions of mankind. It is indeed highly improbable that an utterly wrong idea should have persisted throughout the innumerable centuries since man made his appearance on earth. The admirers of "progress" like to declare that all the ideas they do not approve of, even though they were believed by mankind for so many thousands of years, are mere "superstitions" and "illusions." But these people never care to explain why mankind became the prey of such astonishing superstitions. It is quite true that common opinion is not an absolutely reliable sign of truth; but it is at least a reason for inquiring whether a statement man believed and believes in may not be true. That this statement is not in accordance with some very "progressive" ideas is not at all a proof of its being not true.

The fact, then, that man always believed and still believes in character education, in reform, in improvement—and, of course, in a change for the worse too —may let us suspect that there is some truth in this idea. It will become clear afterwards that there are some very strong, even convincing reasons for accepting this statement. Experience shows that changes of character occur and that they may be brought about by natural influences. Among these influences man's own will and endeavor play quite a prominent part. The opposition against this idea does not arise from facts and from experience but from sources of an entirely different nature.

We need but open our eyes to become aware of the fact that changes of personality are quite common occurrences. History and biography tell us of many cases in which some person became changed so thoroughly that he appeared indeed to have become another personality. We know that a certain habit of life may become—even if it had been adopted consciously and for a definite end at first—a man's "second nature," and that this second nature may replace the first one totally and make it disappear altogether. There is the fact of conversion; there is the other of experience producing a thorough change of personality. The existence of these facts cannot be denied. But these cases are regarded as "exceptions"; such things exist indeed, a man will say, but they are exceptions; exceptions prove the rule, and I, for my part, cannot aspire to be an exception. This argument is, however, logically unsound and untrue from the point of view of psychology. Nobody can know whether he is such an "exception" or not, before having tried to be one. The contention of not belonging to these "exceptional" cases is but a pretext for not trying to be one.

The idea of being incapable of any change is itself part of the character which is in need of change. Everyone feeling in need of change knows by instinct, as it were, that changing is a difficult and a painful task; and human nature tends to escape, as far as possible, all unpleasantness. Paradoxical though it may seem, it is just this conviction of not being able to change which ought to supply a strong reason for attempting to do so.

Why, how, and that human nature, or rather personality, can change will be shown in the subsequent chapters. They have indeed no other intention but to prove this change to be possible and to show the ways promising success. It is, therefore, not necessary to mention here more of the reasons for holding this opinion. Only one fact may be alluded to here. If human character were not susceptible of very great changes, it would be very strange indeed that so many psychologists, pedagogists and philosophers of today deal in their writings just with the problem of character education. During the last thirty years or so numerous treatises have been published on this topic. It is scarcely probable that scholars devote time and attention to an altogether fruitless endeavor and that the public is eager to hear about things of no use at all.

This conviction of the immutability of character has become more general only during the last century. This is curious, because the psychologists of the nineteenth century neglected rather the problems connected with personality and character. One may look through the indexes of many a treatise on psychology—and there are quite a few of them—published between, say, 1870 and 1900, without coming across the terms of character or of the single features of character. Psychology was in those years interested too much in the "elementary" facts of mental life, to care for the complicated phenomena of behavior, character, or personality. The conviction of character being immutable is not, therefore, derived from the facts psychology collected by its experiments and its work done in the laboratories. This conviction is more the result of a general idea of human nature, an idea born of certain philosophies.

The philosophers of the nineteenth century, or at least a great part of them, were so utterly enthralled by the enormous and indeed amazing progress of science that they had come to believe science the only way of understanding reality. This unlucky overrating of science had set in already at an earlier time, but it gained a decisive influence on general mentality only during the last century, after the results of scientific research had become visible to everyone by the progress of technique. Science, however, has to proceed by the way of analysis, by discovering the last "elements" of the complicated phenomena we observe and by reducing these to the most elementary and simple factors. In man the elementary factors seemed to be those of the biological order, the more as physiology hoped to understand human nature by means of physics and of chemistry. Laws of physics, however, are immutable; they cannot be influenced by human will. Human nature becomes immutable if it depends in all its manifestations on the immutable laws of inorganic matter. This trend of thought could not but give rise to the idea of human personality being immutable in the same manner as its basis was thought to be so. But this philosophy overlooked very important and even essential facts. They had to be rediscovered, as it were, and this process of rediscovery which has set in about the year 1900 is not as yet at its end. Modern science had to rediscover the human soul, human liberty, the essential differences existing between a living organism and dead matter, or between mere organic life and the life of the mind. A steadily growing number of scientists, of psychologists, of philosophers turn away from the convictions cherished by the nineteenth century. Though there are still many who will go on believing in the catchwords of those bygone times, those who have become aware that mankind has been ensnared by falsehoods and mistakes gain in influence.

It is not for these pages to describe this change of general mentality to a greater extent and to detail the reasons which have brought it about. But it had to be pointed out that the idea of human personality being essentially immutable is not the result of observation or of experience, much less even of scientific research, but the outcome of very general, and indeed philosophical, ideas. This had to be pointed out the more, because the following chapters will have to allude to general ideas and philosophical views more than once.

3. *I Can Not—I Will Not*

Very often a person will know quite well that he ought to reform or to change and declare himself unable to do so, because of the weakness of his will. This weakness is believed to result from inborn dispositions, physical constitution or immutable temperament. Such a person is quite willing to change—at least he tells us he is—but all his attempts encounter the insurmountable obstacle of his will being too weak.

Exact observation of these people, however, discloses a rather strange fact. The very same person whose will is allegedly too weak for seriously attempting and, even more so, for carrying through any improvement of his moral personality, becomes, under certain circumstances, quite capable of persistence and of an often

amazing power of endurance for hardships. Of this
there are many instances. There is a man whose will is
so weak that he gives way to every unpleasant feeling
resulting from the fatigue and monotony of work; because of this unpleasant feeling he deserts work and prefers the life of the jobless, the vagabond or the beggar;
such a life is anything but an easy one and to support
it one doubtless needs quite a strong will. There is a
boy who has no strength of will when he ought to concentrate on his homework, but his will proves to be
strong enough to make him the head of a gang of
youngsters. Some people have no energy so long as
there is question of work, but they have enough will
left when they have to go through a long and tedious
training for some sport.

From such facts we may gather that strength of will
is not a constant and, as it were, given quantity; it depends very much on the goals proposed to the will. In
St. Augustine's *Confessions* there is a passage very
worthy of becoming the matter of contemplation for all
those who complain of such a weakness of their will.
This passage is doubly interesting, because it is not only
a piece of unrivalled psychology, but also because it is
apparently the first attempt at a psychological analysis
of will known in the history of psychology.

It will be well to quote this passage in full: "I did
then so many things, the willing of which was not the
same as to be able to do them, and yet I did not do that
which pleased me incomparably more, and which I
might be able to do as soon as ever I had the will to do
it. Because, as soon as ever I had the will I should
doubtless be willing, and here the ability is the same as
the will, and the very willing is doing, and yet it was
not done; and the body more easily obeyed the slender-
est will of the soul, by the motion of the limbs, according to its beck, than the soul obeyed itself in procuring

its pleasures, which might be obtained by only willing it. . . .

"Whence is this monstrous thing? And why is it? The soul commands the body, and is presently obeyed; the soul commands itself, and is opposed. The soul commands that the hand should be moved, and it is so quickly executed, that the command can scarce be distinguished from the obedience: and yet the soul is a spirit, and the hand is a body. The soul commands that the soul itself should will a thing, and yet, though it be the same soul, it doth not what is commanded. Whence this monstrous thing, and why is it? It commands, I say, that it should will a thing, which if it did not will already it would never command, and yet that is not done which it commands.

"But it does not entirely will it, and therefore it does not entirely command. For it commands so far only as it wills, and that which it commands is not done, in so much as it does not will. For it is the will that commands that there should be a will, not any other will but itself. It is not then a full will that commands, and therefore that it is not done which it commands; for if there were a full will, there would be no occasion for commanding that there should be a will, for it would be already. It is therefore no monstrous thing, that one should be partly willing and partly not willing, but it is a sickness or weakness of the soul, which, being weighed down by evil customs does not entirely arise when lifted up by truth, and therefore there are two wills, because one of them is not entire, and the one is supplied with what the other needs."

These words of St. Augustine state, in the main, two facts: first, that will and execution are so merged one into the other that it is practically impossible to say where will ends and action begins; this amounts to saying that willing—real willing—and doing are but two sides of one and the same human act. Second, that weakness of will is in truth an illusion or self-deception of the mind, resulting from man's striving for two—or even more—goals at the same time; what is called weakness of will is due not so much to lack of energy as to lack of unity of the will. The trouble lies more with purpose than with will.

Pursuit of two goals at the same time is practically impossible. It becomes pure nonsense when the two goals are quite incompatible with each other. It is already a nearly absolute handicap even when the two goals belong to the same class. All the purposes or aims of man can indeed be grouped into two great classes; man either strives to realize something because it is good in itself, or he does so because it is good for him. The first group comprises more than what is commonly called altruistic ends; altruism applies to all kinds of good referring to other persons; there are, however, non-egoistic ends which have nothing to do with persons, as for instance scientific research. There is also a definite kind of behavior to things; a man may, for instance, be quite patient with people and very impatient with things; he may swear at a lock not opening, lose his temper with his studs, become furious because some other thing does not obey. No other person will gain anything by his giving up these habits, nevertheless he would be right in trying to get his temper in hand, not only because thus he might improve his personality, but also because of the respect due to things.

This imaginary case illustrates an important fact. One and the same goal may be pursued because of different reasons. The man mentioned may try to change because he thinks it wrong to be impatient at all; he may fear that he might sometime behave in this fashion in presence of a stranger; he may consider what has been just called the respect due to things. The effect is the same, though the reasons are very different. Fear of having to be ashamed and consideration of the feelings of others is surely not a bad motive; but it is not an ideal one, nor is it such as ought to prompt our actions. It is still better than mere vanity and the fear of losing reputation. The sameness of behavior is, however, but an apparent one. Closer observation will always reveal some difference in behavior, however subtle, corresponding to the differences of motivation. The way of the vain is not quite the same as the one of the considerate; the man following an impulse towards moral perfection behaves differently from the one who only wants to keep up appearances.

The passage quoted from St. Augustine refers to two wills, one aiming at what reason recognizes as right and true, another to which "custom" draws the mind down. Knowledge of what is objectively better or of a higher value is indeed not a sufficient motive for action. There are more people quite capable of discerning values, than there are who act according to this knowledge. Even those who try to do so very often meet not success but failure. They accuse the weakness of their will, the overwhelming power of habit, the unfavorableness of circumstances, the insufficient education they received —all kinds of things—but not themselves. Summarizing all the obstacles which are opposed to the realization of what they believe to be their real aims, these people declare: I simply can not.

Few words, however, are liable to so much misuse as the two of "I can" and "I will." Thinking or saying: I will do this or that, is not yet a sure sign of real will. A man may say so and believe himself to will, and nevertheless have not more in his mind than just a wish, a yearning that the thing he is thinking of might become real. He may even picture to himself how glad he would be, if this thing came to pass; but it is not more than a dream which creates the illusion of willing, but which has nothing to do even with only the first steps of a true voluntary act. Awakening from his dream, such a man will sigh and be sad, because his dream did not come true, and he will say: Surely it would have been wonderful, but—I can not.

How does he know of this "I can not"? He has not even really tried, and so he is not able to know for sure whether he can or not. And it is not enough to have tried once or several times; one has to try over and over again, because there is always the chance of some opening suddenly being offered to us. This may be the effect of training; it may be also that we overlooked a possibility which had been present since the beginning of our attempts. A new light may dawn on us, and we may be surprised by suddenly being able to do what until now was much too difficult to accomplish. Says Aristotle: "One becomes a mason only by laying bricks and a sculptor only by handling the chisel; even so one acquires a virtue only by exercising it."

The effects of training and exercise are in truth very mysterious, though we usually take them for granted. Common opinion thinks that the fact of our becoming capable of doing something which we could not do before, by training, is "self-evident." But it is with this as it is with many other things we call self-evident, simply because we are accustomed to them, while in truth they are not evident at all but rather amazing and mysterious. If we would but care to think, we would discover among the most trivial things quite a lot of reasons for wonder. The effect of training and repetition is one of these things.

It is indeed quite wonderful that by going over the same passage we at first did not understand at all, or over a mathematical demonstration, we suddenly come to understand it; it is equally wonderful that by doing something we are not able to do perfectly we come to know how to do it. In many of these cases we have been tempted to declare that we "can not" understand or "can not" do the thing; for some reason we went on, and—came to achieve what we thought impossible. It is indeed rather rash to decide that one can not before one has tried quite a lot of times.

Man makes many mistakes in the opposite direction too. He often feels sure of being able to do something he never tried before. Notwithstanding his self-confidence he fails. We overrate easily our capacity for work and for mastering a new situation. Our impression that "we can" may be as unreliable as the other that we can not. Failure often is due to lack of knowledge or to insufficient training. But we fail quite frequently also where no special training is necessary, for instance in social relations. Of these persons failing to establish satisfactory social relations quite a few "feel" beforehand that no good will come from their attempts. Others however are fully convinced of their being charming and lovable, and they expect to get on with their fellows quite nicely. Notwithstanding their conviction they are amazed at finding themselves isolated, out of touch, perhaps respected but not liked, moving as it were on the outskirts and not penetrating into the intimacy of the set they want to belong to. Both types declare, either at the very outset of their attempts, or later on, that they "can not" get really in touch with others. They accuse either circumstances or the lack of amiability in the others, or else some factor, perhaps their own personality, but never in the sense of having made mistakes they could and ought to have avoided. Both of them are probably wrong. There are of course irresponsive people and there are unfavorable circumstances; but they are less frequent than these people who "can not" care to admit. It will be shown in a later chapter how great the rôle of personal attitudes is in these things.

The phrase "I can not" is equivalent very often to the other: "I will not"; but this fact is unknown to the person who feels that he is not able to achieve this or that. The decisive influence of will, though it may be a will hidden to the consciousness of the subject, becomes visible in certain instances. Many people feel that they "can not" say or do things they "want" to say or do. Some person "can not" tell something, not because he is bound to secrecy, but because of some inner inhibition or barrier which does not allow the words to be proffered. The mere physical act of speaking is doubtless the same whatever a man has to tell; it is not more difficult to say: "I have committed murder," than it is to say: "I had yesterday two dry Martinis." It is the consequences which are different. But there are situations in which no consequences of any kind are to be feared; what is told in the confessional is sure to remain there and it is the same with the office of a physician. People, moreover, find it impossible to tell things much less important than a crime. When one gets such a person to tell after all what is on his mind, or when one has been able to guess it, one very often wonders why he did not simply speak out, since there is no reason to be found for his reticence. Sometimes such a person feels quite glad at having told his secret, and very often he himself does not understand why it had been so difficult to divulge it.

There must be, however, some reason for this reluctance against telling certain things; this reason is not to be found in common vanity which recoils from telling things detrimental to the idea others have—or are supposed to have—of this individual's personality. There are, of course, many things a man will be ashamed of telling about himself. But the feeling these reticent people have is more one of repugnance than of shame. But there is a kind of shame which has nothing to do with vanity or even the legitimate desire of hiding things endangering one's social position. This kind of shame springs from the natural and indeed praiseworthy respect for privacy; to reveal certain things without some really cogent reason would justly be called indiscreet. A definite respect is due to our own personality as well as to the personalities of others. But the things people feel unable to tell do not always belong to the class of those discretion forbids to make public; there is, furthermore, no reason for not telling those things under certain conditions, as for instance, in the consultation room of the physician. To explain this reluctance one has to search for still other reasons.

Before attempting to discover these reasons, one does well to remember another phenomenon, which is very frequent and which can be paralleled with the reluctance just mentioned. Here too the attitude of the person is expressed by the phrase: I can not. It is not easy to give to this phenomenon a definite name. Its nature will, however, become clear by some examples.

A woman teacher has been promised an appointment at a larger school and, accordingly, a much higher salary. She would be very grateful for an increase of income, since she has to take care of her old mother. There is but one condition; she has to pass an examination in elementary mathematics. The matter she ought to study is neither large nor difficult nor altogether new to her; one would think that this examination presents no difficulty at all. But the girl declares that she is unable to comply with the conditions, since she "can not" understand even the simplest mathematical demonstration. Though she once had to learn all these things in school, she has forgotten all of them and she has lost, she alleges, all understanding of them. During a series of conversations she had, for some other reason, with a medical psychologist he got her, by some trick, to discuss a problem of mathematics. The question of the eventually impending examination was not mentioned of course. She showed quite a normal understanding. It became manifest that her incapacity of dealing with mathematics existed only in her own imagination. The reasons for not accepting the job offered to her were in fact quite of another nature. The lack of understanding was but a pretext, but one the girl herself felt to correspond to truth. What she really dreaded was not the examination nor to have to study mathematics, but that at her new place she would have to face older girls whose criticism she feared very much. She came from a rather low social class; the school where she was expected to teach was attended mostly by girls belonging to the upper classes. She was not aware of this fear, nor would vanity allow her to become aware of it.

A man, by profession a lawyer, was very fond of literature and used to devote most of his leisure to reading every newly published book he could get. He never dared to mention this hobby in society; he feared that he might forget the name of an author and thus make a very bad impression; if he were to tell about a book and not know its author, he feared to appear stupid. This fear made speaking on books impossible to him, even when he knew the author's name quite well; "I simply can not," he said. The reason for this strange inhibition was indeed fear; but the thing he really feared was not having forgotten a name. He was very ambitious; he knew that his knowledge and judgment in literature was but an amateur's and not equal to that of the specialist. What if he did utter his ideas on literature and there would be present one who really knew about these things? He had to avoid at any cost the possibility of such a discomfiture; but he had also to hide this fear before his own consciousness, because his vanity would suffer by acknowledging the imperfections of his knowledge and judgment.

These two observations have been told here for making clear one important fact. What a person feels that he "can not" may not be the thing he does not want to do; the feeling of an absolute barrier between desire and execution may result from another thing not being willed. Contrary to what is generally supposed the idea of "I can not" is not always so simple a phenomenon. Even letting alone cases verging on pathological inhibition, the inner situation is sometimes much more complicated than one would assume at first sight.

There is a difference between a person who "can not" do something he ought and he wants to do on one side, and a person who "can not" leave things undone he ought not and wants not to do. In a way, it seems easier not to do things, to leave them undone. To do something one needs a special act of will, and nothing can—at least in a normal mind—compel the will to will. Experience teaches, however, that many people find it at least as difficult not to do certain things as to do others. Reference is made often to the power of habit; but even habit, or "custom," as St. Augustine says, is not an invincible force. Nor is it an absolutely sufficient motive; even habit has, to be kept up, to be based on reasons. A man, therefore, who feels it impossible not to do certain things, needs must have some reason for doing them, even though he may not be aware of this fact. These reasons have to be discovered, else no attempt to get rid of the habit will prove successful.

4. *The Difficulties of Self-Knowledge*

Having conceived the idea of improvement being desirable, a man very often will find himself at a loss how to proceed. He does not know where to start. He is ignorant of the means he may employ for realizing his aims. He often does not even see which side of his personality is most in need of reform. He has, if he really desires to make progress, first of all to find out about all these things, then to get a clear idea of the goals he ought to pursue, finally to discover the ways which promise success.

It is commonly said that a man has a better knowledge of himself than any other person ever can have, and that he knows himself better than he knows others. This statement is true in one sense and wrong in another. It is true insofar as everyone, of course, knows what is going on in his mind. He is aware of thoughts he does not care to express, of feelings he carefully hides, of wishes he dares not divulge, things of which others remain ignorant. But the idea of our knowing perfectly our self is wrong insofar as there are ideas at work in our personality, attitudes influencing our behavior, motives regulating our actions, of which we not seldom know nothing at all, and which, nevertheless, may be quite visible to others. There are indeed some good reasons for believing that a man may know more of another's true personality than of his own, and that, accordingly, another may have a better idea of this man's true nature than he has himself.

The entrance to the famous temple of Apollo at Delphi in old Greece, bore an inscription which read as follows: "Know thyself!" Whoever inscribed those words there must have had quite a deep insight into human nature. The words implied that self-knowledge is not a matter of course, not something man simply possesses, but something he has to acquire, or for which he has to strive. The words implied furthermore that special conditions are necessary for acquiring this virtue. We do not arrive at a real knowledge of

ourselves as long as we move in the turmoil of every-
day life; not while transacting business, not while attending to some work, not while studying microscopic
slides, not when merged in the eddy of social intercourse, nor amidst the manifold impressions and activi-
ties of average life can we hope to get a look at our
true personality. We have to withdraw from all this,
to retire into solitude, to seek for a peculiar state of
mind and for congenial surroundings for becoming capable of discovering the truth about ourselves. The ex-
hortation greeting the visitor seemed to imply also that
one has first to know oneself before entering the temple
of the deity, with the intention of praying or asking
for something. Many of the pilgrims who thronged
around the temple had come there to get a prophecy,
an advice, a revelation on the future; but the inscription
seemed to say: It is all right for you to inquire from
the god about the future and the chances of your plans,
but it is much more important that you know yourself.

Far away as we are from these bygone pagan times,
we still do well in paying some attention to the wisdom
of old, not only because Greek speculation is one of
the pillars on which modern civilization rests, and not
only because the Christian Fathers and the Schoolmen
of the Middle Ages very much appreciated the work
of their heathen predecessors, but also because it was in
fact in old Greece that the human mind became first
conscious of its greatest everlasting problems.

The Gospel too suggests that self-knowledge is not a
matter of course, not a knowledge such as we have of
visible and tangible things or of our body and its sensations, not even a knowledge like the one we may
have of another man's faults. A well-known passage
in St. Matthew reads: "And why seest thou the mote
that is in thy brother's eye; and seest not the beam that

is in thy own eye?" We all know this passage, but it can not be said that we act according to it.

The words just quoted admonish us to beware of hasty judgments on our neighbors. We are reminded that we may have faults much greater than those we detect in others. This is, of course, in first line a moral truth. But statements on morals, like this one, very often imply a psychological truth too. If the human mind becomes aware so much more easily of the defects of others than of its own, then it is true that self-knowledge is, as a rule, more difficult to attain than a knowledge of other people. It is not stated by the Scriptural text that our knowledge of others is more reliable than the knowledge of ourselves in every sense; Christ did not teach psychology. But it is averred, in a very definite manner, that in regard to defects our knowledge of ourselves is insufficient and unreliable. But it is precisely about our defects that we have to know as much as possible, if we want to improve at all.

There are still other facts which prove that self-knowledge may not be taken for granted, though common opinion thinks it to be. Children become aware of the feelings, attitudes and the character of other people long before they are capable of forming a definite idea of their own personality. At an age when they are still far from all reflection on their own ego, they know how to pick out, by an often quite surprising intuition, the persons who will behave kindly and understand a child's way; and they avoid others whom they feel to be unkind though these may try to behave in a very friendly manner. The child's mind sees, as it were, through the façade and discovers behind gruffness a kind soul or behind a very sweet mien a callous personality. We have to conclude that the human mind has the gift of perceiving immediately the inner attitudes in another personality, or at least some essential features of it, though this faculty may lose its edge by not being cultivated or by being outweighed by a training in an opposite direction. The existence of this kind of intuition in children proves that a knowledge of other persons may be developed at an age where self-knowledge cannot as yet be thought of.

This knowledge of others, existing in children, is not of course based on a conscious analysis of data; it is not intellectual, but the effect of intuition. If you ask a child why he likes this man and dislikes that one, the child will simply tell you the one is nice and the second is not. The child does not know the reasons for his likes and dislikes.

This intuitional knowledge becomes less when the child grows up; it may even disappear altogether, though in truth no faculty ever disappears really, it is only forgotten or out of training. This loss of intuition is due partly to the influence of environment, partly to that of education. Of environment, because the child soon discovers that his sympathies and antipathies are not always shared by his elders; the child admires them and wishes to be like them and accordingly puts, without noticing it, their judgments in the place of his own ideas. He has been, furthermore, told so often that he does not understand, that his ideas are wrong; therefore he begins to distrust them and is ready to accept those cherished by persons in his environment. Education does not favor the development or the preservation of intuition; the child is trained in the use of the rational faculties and taught to rely on observation and analysis of facts; he learns to trust only so-called objective truth, that is, statements the majority approves of and facts others may verify. Discursive reasoning, syllogistic deductions and inductions become more and more the usual way of thinking, and intuition is accordingly more and more disregarded. But the fact of the intuitional faculty in children is nevertheless a strong argument in favor of the primacy of a knowledge of others.

The loss of this faculty is not parallelized by a corresponding development of self-knowledge. The original understanding of others is not replaced by a growing understanding of one's own self. Man becomes, of course, more and more self-conscious during later childhood and adolescence, but he does not acquire a real and reliable knowledge of himself. His understanding of his own behavior and his own motives—the real ones, not those he believes to determine his actions—remains rather poor.

Only one side of the original power of intuition is still cultivated also in later years—the ability of becoming aware of the faults of one's neighbor.

Another fact which shows our self-knowledge to be rather insufficient is that we are so often surprised by our own actions and thoughts; everyone, probably, has been amazed sometimes by strange thoughts occurring to him and by his acting in a way he never expected to follow. We say in such cases: Well, I never thought myself capable of this. Immoral impulses may arise in our minds and make us afraid of ourselves; we may have imagined that we were quite incapable of hate, and suddenly hate rushes over our mind like a wave. One may feel sure that one will never love or never love again, and suddenly one discovers that one is already in love with someone. More surprising still than the discovery of unthought of feelings is the awareness which sometimes dawns on us of motives we never suspected to be at work in our minds. We believe some action to be altogether unselfish, and suddenly the conviction springs on us that we were prompted by very egoistic motives, or that we did but gratify our vanity when we thought we were obeying objective reasons or striving for objective values.

In such moments we become aware that our knowledge of ourselves is very imperfect. We become apprised, unawares, of forces whose existence we ignored, of motives we deemed out of question, of wishes we recoil from; there are hidden, in some dark recess of our mind, forces for good or for evil of which we knew nothing and which, when let loose, amaze and terrify us by their unsuspected violence.

Considering these facts—and there are so many it would be tedious to mention them here—we must needs conclude that our knowledge of our own mind or our own personality is curiously limited and incomplete and that we are indeed very far from "knowing ourselves best."

Self-knowledge, as it is needed for self-improvement, has to be more than a knowledge of this or that single imperfection or bad habit or faulty inclination. Character and personality are not built up from single bits as a mosaic is built up from single small stones. If some of the stones in such a mosaic are not of the right color or have become cracked, the workman can take them out, throw them away, and replace them by others of the same size; he has only to consider the one stone he is just putting in and the others do not concern him. There is no real connection between the single stones. It is different with a structure like human personality or human character. To describe their peculiarity modern psychology uses the term of "whole."

The essential feature in a whole is the close interrelation of its parts. They are so intimately linked up with each other that they can not even be correctly called "parts." A part has some possibility of separate existence; a single leaf torn out of a book is still something and exists by itself, though it contains often but a meaningless fragment. And a pencil mark on a page or even an inkblot does not destroy the book to which this page belongs. But in a true whole, there is such an intimate connection between the various sides—a term to be preferred rather than "parts"—that none can suffer any influence without all the rest being influenced too, and none is capable of existing by itself, independently of the rest. Because they exist only within the whole they belong to, they all bear the coinage, as it were, of this whole. Intelligence, for example, is not something which exists outside of a person whose intelligence it is; and since every person is an absolutely unique being, every individual's intelligence is individualized too. Psychology describes the general qualities and properties of intelligence; but it cannot grasp the peculiarities which characterize the intelligence of Paul as distinguished from that of Peter.

Nowhere do these properties of a whole become more visible than in human personality. A man is an "individual" in a quite specific sense. Individual signifies that which is not capable of being divided. A heap of stones is no true individual, since it can be divided without losing its identity. A plant is more of an individual; but it is possible, in many cases, to divide it in such a way as to preserve the existence of the parts cut off from the whole; we may plant a twig or a leaf and it will grow roots and develop into a new plant. There are lower animals which we may cut in two parts and each of these parts will go on living and become a complete organism. This faculty of regeneration is missing in more highly developed animals. The lizard may grow a new tail, but the tail does not grow into a new lizard. In birds and mammals even this limited power of regeneration is missing; these animals are, in this regard, more of an individuality than the lower organisms. Indivisibility and, accordingly, individuality become more and more marked as we pass from the lower levels of life to the higher.

Individuality is at its highest, at least so far as this tangible world is concerned, in man who, besides being a living organism, is also a person, that is, a free and reasonable being that is master, up to a certain extent, of its own nature. Personality—in the sense of being a person—is an attribute which belongs to man alone; no animal has personality, and our speaking of the personality of a dog or of a horse has but a figurative meaning. This peculiar faculty of being capable of forming and moulding himself, which man alone among all animals possesses, is indeed the basis of all self-education and self-improvement. Because of this man is in truth responsible for what he is. His personality or his character are not simply given to him like things he has to accept as they are; they are entrusted to him as things he has to complete, to build up and to embellish. Of this, however, more will have to be said in a later chapter.

Individuality penetrates, so to say, deeper into the human person and imbues it more thoroughly than is the case with all other living beings. Every side of a man's person is more his own, so to express it, than the "parts" of an individual of another kind belong to it. The unification or integration peculiar to human nature goes so far that we are not conscious of having any parts; though we speak of our limbs or our memory as if these were distinguishable parts of ourselves, we nevertheless feel our whole being to be an indissoluble unity. We may say: "My leg hurts me," but we may express the same thing by saying: "I have hurt myself on the leg." We say: "My memory fails me," but we do not mean to imply that our memory is a part of our self, which could be separated from this. The phrase "my memory" has quite another connotation than one such as "my pencil." We never say: "My memory re-members" or: "My reason understands"; it is our own self that remembers and understands.

It is the same with features of character. Though we say this man's sense of duty or that other one's pride, we do not mean to imply that sense of duty or pride are things which could be separated from the person we credit with these qualities. The pride of one man is not the same thing as the pride of another; every char-acter-trait, though we have to call it by the same name, is something quite individualized, something peculiar, something personal, to say the least, in every single per-sonality.

The many terms language puts at our disposal are general names. We cannot name an individual as such. If we want to give it a name we have either to choose a proper name—of a person, a town, a mountain—or find some other way of designating it, as: the tailor at the corner, the mountain we climbed together last summer, the capital of the state of Illinois. Proper names or their substitutes correspond to gestures by which we point out a thing or point at the thing. Proper names are in fact of a "demonstrative" character, to be used whenever we are not able to point at the thing or the man we have in mind. All names which are not proper names may be used also in connection with an indefinite article: a mountain, a town, a man. A general name can never exhaust the peculiarities of an individual. Even if we try to describe an individual as completely as possible by enumerating all its properties, something very important still remains unsaid, namely, the mys-terious quality, or whatever else it has to be called, which makes out of this union of properties a unity and an in-dividuality. Individuals cannot be expressed by words, philosophy tells us.

Because of this fact that individuals are inexpressible

and because every quality of an individual bears the quite unique stamp of the same individuality, these qualities elude equally full expression in language. Peter's pride is not the same as Paul's, as has been remarked before.

These statements seem to be rather abstract and very theoretical. They have nevertheless an immediate bearing on very practical questions. The considerations on individuality lead to a very important conclusion which may be expressed this way: there is no "dictionary of symptoms." That is to say that the "same" quality or the "same" feature of behavior may have quite a different signification when observed in one person and when occurring in another. It may even assume a different meaning in one and the same person at different periods of his life.

We do not perceive directly the features of character. We become aware of them by observing the behavior of a person and by interpreting it. We do not see vanity, but certain actions we believe to result from vanity. By calling a man proud we do not imply that we are able to see his pride as we see the color of his hair, but that certain of his actions seem to derive from pride. In our judgment on character there is always a great deal of interpretation. This ought not to be forgotten, though it is unhappily often neglected.

It is a sad fact that most men are conscious of these facts whenever being so may result in a disadvantageous opinion in others, but not when it may give rise to a more lenient judgment. We hear of a kind action, and instead of being glad of it, we begin to doubt whether it has been really kindness which prompted the deed; we hear of an action we disapprove of, and we are quite sure that there is no other explanation. We remember but too well that appearances may be deceiving in the case of a good action, but we are generally oblivious of this principle when judging an apparently bad action.

It will be shown later that behavior or some feature of it is liable to many explanations and that, great as the similarity of the behavior of different people may be, the motivations giving rise to this behavior may be not at all of the same kind in the single instances.

It is therefore not enough for a man wanting to improve that he knows what mistakes he usually makes, what faults he is given to committing, what bad habits he is indulging in; to know all this is but the beginning of self-knowledge. But true knowledge of one's self means also, and even particularly, a knowledge of the motives behind the single undesirable qualities. So long as he does not grasp fully the background of his behavior, he will hardly be able to get rid of his faults. This is the reason why so many people who are fully aware of their bad qualities and sincerely wish to get rid of them do not make any noticeable progress.

It is not always easy to find out about the real reasons of behavior. To understand these difficulties, one has to recall that every action—whether by deeds or by words—has a threefold meaning. It means first its immediate object: a sentence means what it says, an action what it is intended to achieve. If I say: it is a rainy day, the fact that there are clouds in the sky, that the air is damp, the soil wet, etc., is the meaning of my words. If I wind up my watch, its going the next day, supplying the knowledge of time, is the meaning of my action. But in the words I speak and in the deeds I do there is another side too. Partly in what I say or do, partly in the manner I speak or act, my whole inner attitude, the mood I am in this very moment, find their expression. Speech and action change, for instance, when I am in a hurry, or angry, or tired; they are different when I am paying careful attention to them and when I behave in a more casual way; different when I feel depressed or when I am in good spirits. Our actions and words disclose to an attentive observer a good deal of our inner life. They are, besides meaning a thing or being directed towards the realization of an aim, expressions of what is going on in our mind. In some cases, which are not the rule but nevertheless very frequent, we become conscious of our actions and words "betraying" our feelings or our intentions; we have to be careful so as not to let another guess at our true state of mind. We may also make use of this fact and let another know what we are feeling or thinking without having to put this into words; the inflection of the voice, the position of the head, the expression of the face, etc., may convey a perfect intelligence. But human actions have still a third side. Nearly all our words are spoken and many of our deeds are done with the intention of eliciting some answer or some reaction from another person. Professor Buehler, the distinguished psychologist of Vienna, to whose ideas this discussion on signification is largely indebted, calls this side of behavior, especially of speech, the one of "appeal." When we tell a friend what we think of a certain matter, we expect him to share our opinion or, at least, to be interested; when we ask him a question, we expect him to answer; when we utter a wish, we expect him to act accordingly. Most human actions are determined by man's social nature; of course there are many which are not immediately connected with being a member of a family, a citizen of a country or belonging to human society or to some religious community. But some relationship, to other people, even though indirect, is never absent; we act in a way which will gain approval or we avoid acts we know to be discreditable, and thus take account of common opinion. Most of our work brings us directly or indirectly in touch with other people; it is destined for them, paid by them, arranged according to their wants; it has to satisfy them, that is, to elicit a response of approval. The majority of all our actions has therefore to be considered from three different points of view; we have to distinguish meaning, expression and appeal.

Each of these three sides of action gives rise to a peculiar kind of misunderstanding. We may be mistaken in catching the meaning of words or the true aims of actions; we may misinterpret the expression conveyed by them; we may react in a manner not corresponding to the intentions of the person speaking or acting.

All three kinds of misunderstandings are very frequent and become easily the source of many troubles and difficulties. Not to be understood, because I can not make my meaning sufficiently clear, because I can not make the other person see the point, because he is unable to follow my thoughts, or to detect the true meaning of my actions, is as troublesome as not understanding him. Mutual understanding is the basis of society and co-operation. Sometimes two people behave as if they spoke different languages, though they both use plain English. It has been said that men are islands shouting to each other across a sea of misunderstanding. This is indeed true in quite a few cases, though there are plenty of exceptions too.

These misunderstandings are, however, not as frequent and not as dangerous as those arising from a wrong interpretation in regard to expression. The words may be so clear and the actions so simple that another can not fail to grasp their meaning; but we can always ask whether this meaning corresponds really to what is in the mind of him who so acts or speaks. We may always be at a loss as to what is "behind" them.

It is hardly necessary to illustrate by examples the

manifold interpretations which one simple fact may suggest. A man is sent on an errand; he of course surmises that the thing he is told to do has to be done or is needed by him who sent for it; but he may also think that the other wanted him to be out of the way for some more or less disreputable reason. Jealousy is, for instance, very much inclined to seek for the second interpretation, and it is wrong oftener than not. Someone enters a room whose two occupants cease to speak at that very moment; this may be a mere accident; it may be because they discussed a confidential matter the third is not entitled to know; it may be that the topic they had chosen is quite uninteresting for the uninitiated; but it is also possible that the newcomer had furnished the topic of their conversation. The interpretation one places on the behavior of his fellows depends nearly exclusively on one's ideas or prejudices; they determine one's opinion much more than do objective facts.

Preconceived ideas, which quite often are not at all conscious, influence human behavior to an extent generally very much underrated. They determine the attitudes of people in politics, in matters of faith, against their neighbors, on behalf of their convictions so much, that one not seldom doubts whether objective opinions exist at all. The rôle of prejudice is indeed enormous. Everybody would do well, for that matter, to peruse carefully Cardinal Newman's remarks on prejudice and on assumed principles (in his *Lectures on the Present Position of Catholics in England*, Lectures VI and VII). The study of these passages ought to prove very useful for understanding other people and ourselves.

Man judges all things, all actions, all events from his personal point of view. In many a respect he does not know where he in fact stands. His "standpoint" is hidden to him; he cannot see it, because he is standing on it. But it is very important to know exactly where one stands, because the view one gets of things depends not only on their shape, but very much on the perspective they present when looked at from a particular point. A landscape, a building, every object may look quite differently when viewed from one side or from another. It is the same with mental things, with ideas, with opinions, with the image we form of our neighbor's actions and character. It is the same with the idea we have of our own personality. We can walk around a building and get the impression it makes when viewed from all sides; we may try to get an objective image of a man's behavior by conscientiously going over all possible ways of interpreting it; but we can not do the same thing with our own personality. We can not walk, as it were, round our own self. We carry the point of view, the point on which we stand, with us; we may discover many things, but not this point. Even by changing our point of view we can never be sure of having got a better or a clearer image of ourselves, because we never really know the peculiarities of the point on which we stand and, accordingly, of the view it affords.

In every attempt at self-knowledge the observer and the observed are one and the same; the actor is at the same time the public. This is the tremendous difficulty and the great danger of self-knowledge.

We have to look into a mirror for the sake of discovering what our face is like. But we never see, unless we make use of a special arrangement, our face as it is and as the others see it, because the mirror shows on our right side what in fact is on the left and vice versa. Nobody's face is so symmetrical that it remains unaltered by exchanging its halves. This is, for that matter, the reason why most people feel dissatisfied by pictures which have been taken of them, even when others declare these pictures to be perfect as to likeness. Nobody is used to seeing himself as the lens pictures him; for knowing whether the picture is right or not, one has to put it before a mirror. We see ourselves indeed "through the looking-glass," that is in a rather unreal manner.

5. How to Know Oneself

To know oneself is not easy. This may seem a rather paradoxical statement, since according to general belief everyone knows himself best. But one needs, in fact, quite a technique and, as it were, a special training, if one really wants to know oneself.

That this is the case has been known to the wizards of all ages. Mention has been made already of the inscription at Delphi. Another fact worthy of consideration is the following. It seems to have been, and to be, a general conviction among the teachers of true wisdom that to attain perfection man has to find a teacher or a leader who controls the steps of the beginner, warns him of the mistakes he makes, and points out to him the pitfalls besetting his way to progress. Progress is not possible without self-knowledge; but to attain this, the advice of a master and a special technique seem to be indispensable. The idea of a "spiritual director" is not a peculiarity of Catholicism, though, of course, confession as a sacrament is. Chinese, Mahommedan or Indian wisdom recommends that a man desirous to advance on the road to progress ought to choose a "director."

This advice implies the idea, alluded to in the last chapter, that another person may eventually know more about one's personality than does this person himself. The first thing for attaining real and reliable self-knowledge seems, therefore, to be that one learn to look at one's own self in the objective and dispassionate way of another person.

The observer cannot perceive immediately what is going on in the mind of the person he studies. All he observes are this person's behavior, his actions, his gestures, his words, the inflections of his voice, the expression of his face. All this he sees, it is true, not quite in the same way as he sees the other visible things, because he knows beforehand that every word and every action has a definite meaning and that it is an expression of what is going on in the mind. The things he observes are more than just visible facts, they are "signs" of something else. This we know without having accumulated any previous experiences; this knowledge is part of our original endowment. A certain understanding of signs is found already in some animals, especially in those living in groups or herds. But this faculty is very limited and there are but very few and simple signs. Knowing something for a sign and understanding what is signified by it, are, however, two very different achievements. There are some signs in whose signification we cannot well be mistaken; for example, a gesture pointing at something is generally understood. But even signs which at first sight seem to be quite univocal may have, according to circumstances, several meanings, or they can be given quite another signification by some slight modification. To grasp this fact one has but to remember the many shades of laughter and smile: joy, disappointment, irony, malice, triumph, shame, despair, doubt and some other sentiments too may find expression by laughing or smiling.

The peculiar process by which we become aware of the meaning of a sign has been alluded to already; it is called interpretation. Its results may be right, they may also be quite wrong. A good many of the difficulties we experience in dealing with other people and of the troubles which make life a burden arise from wrong interpretations. It is indeed sometimes not easy to discover the real meaning of a person's behavior. To understand a person thoroughly one has to be able to look at the world, at things, at people, at situations exactly from the point of view this person holds; to know this point of view one has to be very well acquainted with this person's history, his antecedents, his nearer and his farther goals, his momentary mood and his habitual temperament. This being the case, one rather wonders at the lightmindedness and rashness of some people who pass judgments on their fellows without caring for sufficient information. Our opinions of other people are, moreover, very much influenced by our own prejudices, preferences, likes and dislikes, by our own interests and moods; they are therefore often very far from being objective and reliable.

There is, therefore, no guarantee that the opinions others have formed of our own personality are true so far as to afford us a trustworthy idea of what we are. If a man would ask several of his acquaintances what they believe him to be, the answers would be—provided they are sincere—very different. Notwithstanding these drawbacks, the opinions of others on ourselves may be rather useful, if we only came to know them. Generally we are not apprised of what others think of us; but when we become, by chance, aware of their opinion we do not believe it to be true, especially when it diverges much from what we think or when it is not complimentary enough. People tell what they think of each other usually only in a fit of temper; and this may indeed distort their opinion.

By paying some attention to casual remarks of our fellows we may, however, guess at their opinions. We will probably disbelieve them, feel offended by them, think of ourselves as misjudged and as badly treated—

seldom will we feel that they overrate us—we will call them clumsy idiots, incapable of true understanding, yet it is worth while to give their ideas some consideration. We might at least ponder on them a little and inquire whether there is not a grain of truth in them. Distorted as our image may appear in this mirror, there will still be something of our shape to be discerned.

More reliable than their remarks is the general behavior of our neighbors. It reflects the impression our own conduct makes on them. They do not, as a rule, trouble to analyze our character, or to make a special study of it. They do not even have, very often, a clear idea of what we are. But they have one nevertheless, clear or dim, according to which they fashion their behavior.

Strange though it may appear at first sight, the behavior of our neighbors depends much more on our real and unspoken motives, even on motives we ourselves are not conscious of, than on those we believe to be at work in our minds. This can be gathered from the same kind of observations on children which were used already before to prove the existence of an original intuition of another personality. A child still naïve, natural, untainted by conventions, in possession of his unspoiled instincts will, for instance, refuse to make friends with a stranger though he may try very hard to be kind and friendly; the child somehow sees through such a man's behavior and feels this kindness and friendliness to be only perfunctory, to be untrue, a mere mannerism and hiding in fact a callous and unkind personality. Or a child will seek the company of a man apparently gruff and cold, because the child's intuition is aware of a truly kind mind hidden beneath the rough surface.

Education and the observance of the rules of social life indeed overlay, as it were, this natural and primitive intuition. But no original faculty disappears really;

it goes on functioning, even though man is not conscious of it. The attitudes of men towards each other depend much more on unconscious knowledge of another's motives than one would care to assume.

It is for this reason that the behavior of others, as dictated by their more or less unconscious opinion, becomes interesting in regard to the approach to self-knowledge; this is true especially of those who are friendly-minded towards us, and those who belong to the inner circle of our acquaintances. Whenever the behavior of a friend, of one who likes us and whom we like, denotes something like resentment or that he is about to withdraw, we ought to take account of this as a danger signal. But even the behavior of our friends —and in a way of our enemies too; they can be sharp-sighted enough—affords not more than just a platform from which to start. The real work has still to be done.

To get a trustworthy idea of ourselves we have to try for an objective and dispassionate image, free as far as possible from prejudices, from all overrating vanity so easily leads to, and from all underrating too which results very often from unsatisfied ambition. We have to discard what we used to think of ourselves and to look at our personality with the cool eye of the scientist studying a strange animal. We have to try to form an opinion more impersonal, more objective even than the one others may have formed. We have to make a diagnosis of our own self after the manner of a physician. This is indeed a very difficult task, and an unpleasant one too. We have to face all the things we used to look away from, to dig up all kinds of memories we were but too happy to forget, to confess to ourselves all we had carefully hidden in the depths of our minds. As the famous German philosopher Immanuel Kant somewhere remarks, the ascent to the Divine leads through the hell of self-knowledge.

There is but one way for attaining a reliable idea of self. If we want to know what another man is really like, we study his actions and his whole behavior. We have to do the same thing with our own life. In doing this we have to discard all knowledge of our motives, our ends, our thoughts and our feelings. Not as if they were without importance; far be it from us that we fall into the error of those so-called psychologists, the behaviorists, who believe that psychology has no other task than describing behavior. This is in fact no psychology at all, or if it is, it is just an introductory chapter. There will be a time to deal with the conscious contents of our mind too; but we have to begin with an analysis of behavior. And to know exactly what our behavior is like we have to turn our attention to the effects produced by it in reality.

Many will probably find fault with the statement that our actions reveal more of our true personality than do thoughts and feelings and intentions and what not besides. Our best intentions, they say, are often frustrated by factors altogether independent of our will; unfavorable circumstances, things we were unable to foresee, mistakes we unwillingly make have a very great influence on the effects of our actions. If by chance I hurt someone while throwing pebbles into a river, this is doubtless an effect of my action; but this effect cannot be attributed to my doing, since I am not to be held responsible. Maybe; but maybe also I ought to have considered this possibility of hurting someone and that I neglected to do so, because I was so intent on having my pleasure. Whether the factors influencing the effect of our actions really are quite strange to our personality, has to be found out first; there is always the presumption that we may be party to them. Our not having foreseen the results is often out of the question; but it might still be asked whether we ought not to have foreseen. Many people indeed do not see what they do not want to see. Whether the effects of a man's behavior are due exclusively or partly to factors independent of his personality can be found out only by a careful analysis; it is impossible to give an offhand answer to this question.

The notion of the effects or results of our actions needs some further discussion. When speaking of the effects of some action a man generally has in view only to realize the goal which he had planned for his action; by a bad result he means that things did not come out as he thought they would, and by a good result that they came out according to his plans. A good result is more or less identified with success, a bad one with failure. This way of judging actions may be all right in many respects; it is insufficient for the purpose of self-analysis.

The common idea of result is indeed too narrow. An action has more effects than the one it is planned for. To explain this, it will be useful to borrow a term from the technical language of chemistry; the chemist calls certain substances which are formed besides the one he is intent upon "by-products." It is about the same with human actions; they are intended to bring about a certain result, but they have "by-effects" too. This fact is well-known in theory; in practice man's mind is so much enthralled by the goal he is after that the "by-effects" are neglected altogether. A man speculating in stocks is intent only on his gain; the loss of the opposite side does not matter to him. If he thinks of it at all, he looks at it as an inevitable feature of speculation or as a proof that others have been clumsy, while he proved to be the better man. A scientist will devote all his time and perhaps more money than he can afford, to the pursuit of some research work; he overlooks completely the fact that he is neglecting his wife, becoming a stranger to his children, that he misses many things and gives up many of his chances for happiness. He need not be a bad man, not even an egoist; his work may be quite disinterested; but there are nevertheless some rather undesirable "by-effects" of his behavior. A person may be driven by what is indeed an unruly and badly employed love of truth to tell the truth everywhere and to everyone, whether asked to do so or not; he is quite proud of his truthfulness, and he does not notice that he offends many people, that he causes unnecessary troubles, that he has neither tact nor true love in his soul.

For the sake of analysis all effects of an action, whether immediate or remote, whether essential or only accidental, have to be considered. Account has also to be taken not only of what is done, but also of how it is done. One and the same action can be executed in various ways. One may, for instance, ask for a favor in a friendly or an unkind, a bashful or an exacting, in a polite or a rude manner. The same holds good of granting a favor. The French have a saying: *c'est le ton qui fait la musique*, it is the sound that makes music, which means that not the words or the actions of a man, but the way they are spoken or done will reveal what really is in his mind.

We would get a wrong idea of the structure of the human mind, were we to believe that the goal man consciously pursues needs must supply the real motive of his actions. A man may persuade another to follow a certain line of action, or, maybe, only to take another way while walking, and believe that he is doing so because the way he proposes is surer or better or shorter, which indeed may be quite true; but his real motive may be that he wants to impose his will, that he wants to show that he knows better, and so on. This becomes visible, for instance, when such a man insists on taking a short cut, though there is no reason for hurrying. He still will believe—really believe, not only pretend—that to take the shortest way is the reasonable thing to do; but his real motive is quite a different one. He will be unable to discover his real motives unless he considers not only the immediate effect of his action—needing less time for the way—but the more remote too, namely, that another man is forced to do his will.

By this he will become acquainted with the aim he is in truth pursuing. It is the aims which determine the quality of an action. An aim is pursued, because the result of its realization is believed to be in some sense "better" than another state of things. Man acts only because he feels the actual state of things to be unsatisfactory and because he hopes that his action will bring about a better state. A man about to deliver a speech puts his watch on the pulpit, because it seems better placed there before his eyes than to be placed in his pocket and to have to be drawn out from time to time. A man leaving his home for a walk gazes at the sky and goes back to get his umbrella; it is better, he says, to take the umbrella than to get wet. An author strikes out a word in his manuscript and changes it for another, because this seems to express his mind better or to sound better. A person deliberating on several lines of action open to him, decides for one of them, saying: This is the best way, I guess. What one thinks the "best" is revealed by one's actions, whether this choosing the best has been a conscious process or not.

No word is, perhaps, so much misused as "will." There is often a long way from purpose to action, but the way from will to execution is very short or, rather, it does not exist at all, as St. Augustine rightly points out. This statement seems incredible to many people. They remember so many instances of having been willing to do something and not having done it nevertheless. They have heard, moreover, plenty of talk on strong and on weak will, they know that their own will is sometimes stronger and sometimes weaker. They feel very energetic when they are well, and deprived of energy when their health is a little impaired. From this they conclude that there must be differences in the strength of will. But if they cared for a more close analysis, they would find out that things stand in truth differently. When they do not feel well, they want definitely to have nothing to do, to keep quiet, to take a rest, to do only what can help them to get well again. These are the goals of the "other will" St. Augustine speaks of, which goals enter into competition, as it were, with those proposed, be it by duty or else by some appeal coming from without. It is not that the strength of their will has suddenly become less; it is that their will has lost its unity, that a second will has entered into play which often proves able to prevail over the first. Weak will is divided will; this fact one has to keep in mind for understanding many of the otherwise unintelligible features of human behavior.

Some remarks have to be added on habit. Man attributes to habit many actions which he feels he has not consciously decided on. We do indeed many things without previous deliberation or even without thinking of them, because doing so has become a habit with us. No need to decide expressly that we have to dress or to comb our hair or to use a fork at meals. But the fact of a habit having come to be established does not exclude decision and will altogether. Decision has been made, so to say, once and for all; we have learned that this or that behavior is right and we were, and are, willing to do the right thing. The observation of habit or the obedience to it results from a foregone decision; this becomes obvious in a phrase like this: "I have made it a rule. . . ." Making a rule means having

decided that one will, from now on, act in a definite
manner whenever a certain situation arises. It makes
no difference whether this rule has been consciously
stated or whether it has been adopted under the influence of training or education or some other factor, for
example, adjustment to custom. Decisions a man made
can be unmade again. What has been acquired by training can be given up again by a training opposed to the
first. No habit is endowed with an irresistible force;
if a man, wanting to get rid of a habit, is unable to do
so, it is not because habit is irresistible, but because he
still clings to the aims this kind of action realizes. The
resistence habit opposes to the attempts of giving it up
does not depend on the length of time this habit existed
and not on its peculiar nature—at least these factors are
not the really decisive ones—but on, so to say, how
much the person loves and cherishes this habit.

We have, for the sake of finding out the truth about
ourselves, to consider at first all our actions and all our
behavior as if it depended exclusively on our choice
and our free will. Only after having pushed forward
this analysis as far as we can, are we allowed to assume
an influence exercised by factors alien to personality.
To repeat it once more: this statement does not exclude
all influence of factors independent of will; it declares
only that we can not discover their influence but by a
process of exclusion, determining first the rôle played
by will. We are sure to discover that this rôle is much
more important than we used to think.

It is not a pleasant idea that many of the difficulties
we have to wrestle with are of our own doing. We may
not be wholly responsible for them, since we are not
conscious of what we were doing. The fact remains,
however, that the causes of a great many of our troubles
lie within our own self. Painful as this may be, it is
nevertheless true. But man tries to escape from all

painful sensations as far as possible. Every explanation which takes from him responsibility or even the faintest trace of it are welcome. It is for this reason that the idea of character being determined mainly by heredity meets such applause. But this question deserves to be discussed in a separate chapter.

6. *On Personality and Character*

Many people know that they have this or that undesirable quality or habit, and they would be quite glad to get rid of it; but they believe this to be impossible, because this quality is, as they say, part of their nature; they were born with it, they cannot help being what they are, any more than they can help having blue eyes or brown.

These people appeal, for proving their point of view, to the fact that they have tried many times and very hard to give up the habit which worries them; they failed and therefore feel sure that it can not be done. But experience as such does not prove anything so long as one is not quite sure of having employed the best method. Negative arguments have no conclusive force; it is only the positive argument that counts. One single case of thorough change of character is quite sufficient to disprove once and for all the idea that character is immutable; but one hundred thousand cases of no change having been attained is no proof for the contrary statement.

Changes of character doubtless occur. There are some well-known cases of conversion in which a man not only turned from unbelief to belief, or from one faith to another, but became so thoroughly changed, so absolutely another personality that those who had known him before were hardly capable of recognizing him. Certain experiences may condition a deep-seated change of character; betrayal, disappointment, misfortune or a stroke of luck may work this way. A callous miser may become a loving and charitable being, like Mr. Scrooge in Dickens' *Christmas Carol*—and such things do not occur in fiction only—and a trusting and friendly character may change into a suspicious and misanthropic one. Psychopathology knows of certain cases, commonly described as of "multiple personality," which prove that one human being can present successively and alternately several very different types of character.

Experience and environmental factors cannot condition a change of innate faculties nor can they influence the constitution of the organism. A person of a definite body-build and a definite hereditary constitution may develop more than one character. These cases, though abnormal, are not cases of brain trouble; the bodily health is quite untroubled, the nervous system is quite intact; the arising of a new character is the effect of purely mental influences. Under normal conditions too, mental influence may give rise to a rather surprising change of character; mental treatment results sometimes in producing a character very different from the one the patient showed before. In these cases also there is no question of cerebral trouble; nor can any alteration of the bodily structure, the constitution or the hereditary endowment result from mere psychical influence. This being the case, there is evidently a chance that mental influence brought to bear on a normal mind, may end in changing the character and in helping a man to get rid of undesirable habits and qualities.

It seems advisable to state first what the meaning of the terms we constantly use really is. In common language, and even unluckily in scientific psychology, the terms of person, personality and character are used promiscuously; the effect is a great confusion and quite a number of misunderstandings. It is not for these pages to discuss the various meanings attributed to the terms mentioned by the various psychologists; nor can it be hoped that common language may be made to care for a more precise use of them. But it will be well to fix the meaning given to them in the course of the present discussions.

A new-born child, then, is a complete person; that is, he possesses all the qualities he ever will or can show; no new quality is added to this original endowment in later years. The nature of a human individual is fully determined by the soul which, as the principle of physical and mental life, develops mere matter into a living organism and a reasonable being. Many of those qualities are, of course, still undeveloped in the new-born infant and during childhood; they appear only later, but to appear they must have been present somehow in a latent state before. Philosophy speaks of them as existing in the state of potentiality and becoming actualized, that is, real and efficient, at a later time. Human nature, being absolutely determined by the individual soul, remains unchanged the whole life. Nothing can add any quality or take away one from the original endowment, though certain circumstances may make it impossible for a quality, existing still in potentiality, to become manifest, or make disappear again one already having become actual. The individual nature existing in reality, including all the actual and the potential features, is called person. It is the same during the whole life; the same in the child and in the adult; the same in health and in disease. The person is essentially immutable. Qualities appear or disappear, but the substratum in which they exist remains the same. A striking illustration of this fact is supplied by observations on cases of a certain disease of the brain, called progressive paresis. This disease gives rise to what appears to be a destruction of qualities; intelligence, social behavior, shame, feelings, memory seem to have disappeared altogether. But sometimes the destructive process going on in the brain can be made to regress; since the discovery of the fever-cure by Professor Wagner von Jauregg, of the university of Vienna, medicine has learned how to deal with such cases. When this cure has been efficient one sees all the apparently destroyed qualities and character-features reappear again. They must, therefore, have gone on existing, though they did not become manifest, the brain trouble not allowing for their manifestations.

The person, then, is complete from the very moment when the soul joins the body. (The exact nature of this union of the soul and body cannot be discussed here; and the philosopher will have to condone the vagueness of the expressions used in this respect.) The person does not become richer in qualities, nor poorer. The qualities it has been given originally may stay on in the state of potentiality, or they may become actualized and real. The actualization of the potentialities depends on several factors. Some of these are inherent in the individual, part are extraneous to it. To the first group belong the laws of evolution, according to which certain features appear at a certain age, for instance, sexual maturity. The second group of factors comprises all environmental influences actualizing the potentialities of the individual; environment cannot produce anything new, it can only develop into real existence what already existed potentially. The faculty of speech, for instance, is an essential feature of human nature, but it does not develop spontaneously; it needs to become actual, the environmental influence of speaking people; the child must hear speech and be spoken to in order to learn to speak himself. Deaf mutes and children who by some misfortune have been shut off from human society, do not speak, though the faculty of speech is of course present and will be brought into action as soon as the necessary stimulation comes from without.

Even in the adult there are still many features not yet actualized. The common idea that after a certain age has been reached no further development is possible, is surely wrong. There are many instances of older people developing hitherto unknown features of character or of acquiring faculties they had not shown before. Here again all depends on the method employed; it is true that older people usually do not change nor develop new faculties; but the negative instances are more than outbalanced by the positive ones. Many older people would quite easily learn a new thing, say a new language, if they were not handicapped by the common conviction that they never will be capable of such an achievement. The sum-total of the actual faculties or qualities is probably never equal to the totality of those which could become actual.

Man perceives only what is actual; he can guess at potentialities and does so; but he can never touch or see them. The image we have of a man is based on what has been actualized in his person. This is what the term "personality" is meant to signify. Personality, accordingly, is the name we give to the sum-total of actual features of a person. Personality can undergo many changes; it develops during childhood, it shrinks in disease or old age. After maturity has been reached, personality does not change very much in average cases; but this does not amount to saying that change is impossible.

Man does not exist in isolation. He is always part of a world which surrounds him, which acts on him and on which he reacts. The world gives rise to impressions, impressions lead to thoughts, thoughts engender action, and action causes some, however slight and passing, change in the perceptible world, and thus causes new impressions. There is an everlasting flux and reflux, starting from the world and returning to it, after having passed through the human mind. The way men act and react depends largely on the idea they have of the world. Every action aims, as has been explained before, at the realization of some value; of something which is believed to be "better." The way of action is, therefore, determined in first line by the ideas of better and worse a man has developed. These ideas become the principle by which he acts. It is as if everyone were obeying some rule stating what has to be preferred and what has to be rejected.

Character is revealed by actions. When trying to find out the character of a person we do not rely on his words alone; we try to get a complete knowledge of his behavior in various situations. Thus we obtain an idea of his character. The actions of a man are of many different kinds; but we trust that they will, whatever aim they are directed to, reveal the character. Character is, accordingly, nothing else but this general rule of principle of behavior; this principle is based on the idea one has of the order of values. We may define character as the common principle underlying a man's actions, which principle refers to values.

Character has to be distinguished from personality. To the latter belong also features which are not to be subsumed to character, as for instance, all that is called temperament. The relation of character to person and personality may be stated as follows: A person acts by the means of his personality according to his character. The latter, depending as it does on ideas of value, is essentially mutable. Since character is no rigid, unchangeable structure it cannot be considered as the necessary and inevitable result of hereditary factors.

This is not tantamount to stating that heredity plays no rôle at all in the formation of character or the development of personality. There is indeed a definite importance of hereditary factors too; but this influence has to be properly evaluated. This is the more necessary as today there is a controversy raging between two extreme parties, the one attributing character exclusively to heredity, the other claiming environment to be the only determining influence. Extreme ideas are bound to be wrong. Neither the advocates of heredity nor those of environment take a sufficient account of facts. Inherited features exist at first merely as potentialities; some actualizing factor is needed to transform them into actualities. These actualizing factors are not always inherent in human nature, as has been shown in the case of the faculty of speech. Environmental influences have to be added to hereditary endowment for personality to develop. Environmental factors, on the other hand, can gain influence only if there is already a certain faculty for reacting on them; they can bring forth only what exists already as a potentiality within the person. The truth about environment and heredity as determining personality and character has to be sought for in a middle line.

The extreme theories, moreover, forget a very important fact. They both consider human nature as if it were subjected to the laws of heredity or environment in a merely mechanical fashion; they neglect altogether the fact that man is free and capable of determining himself. Personality and character are not things simply "given" to man, things he has to reckon with, but on which all influence is denied to him. Personality and character are, to an unsuspected extent, man's own work, and to build them up is a task devolving on man. This capability of moulding itself, of gaining influence on what it is and what it becomes, of conforming to ideals and being what it ought to be is an essential feature of human nature.

The theories of heredity and environment have been worked out by biologists, physicians, psychologists, sociologists, in short by men of science. Science, however, is subjected to the influence of the general mentality of its time. The theories spoken of here arose during the nineteenth century and they bear the stamp of the materialistic way of thought characteristic of this age. Mere facts remain of course untouched by the changes of general mentality; the interpretation they are given, however, is very much influenced by this mentality. It is difficult for the layman and sometimes even for the specialist, to find out what in a given statement is a mere description of a fact and what belongs to interpretation, since the facts are usually stated in the language of a definite theory. Human nature longs much more for explanation than for facts; we want to know why things are and why they are thus. The theories and interpretations given by the scientists become, therefore, much more influential than the naked facts. Theories which fit in with the general trend of mentality are more easily believed by the public than are those contrary to the generally accepted ideas. A mostly materialistic era like the nineteenth century, accepted gladly theories of a materialistic coinage. An idea, however, which has once become rooted in the mind of the public is apt to be rather persistent. Even though the ideas of the scholars may change—and in truth they do change oftener than is generally believed—the public will go on believing what it has been told. This inertia of general belief is, in a way, quite a happy fact. Life would become quite difficult and uneasy if everyone did change his mind as often as science has to change its views. But this inertia becomes, on the other hand, a nuisance, because general mentality will hold on, with a noticeable pertinacity, to ideas science has had to reject.

There is, however, a special reason why the theory that character is due exclusively to heredity has met such an approval and why it is not discarded, though it is evidently disproved by facts. The idea that character is determined by the inexorable laws of heredity supplies in fact an all too welcome pretext for not attempting any change. Laziness and unwillingness for strenuous action finds an apparently valid excuse in this theory. It is indeed more pleasant to imagine character and personality as beyond the reach of human will and of human exertion, than to think of them as entrusted to us, as something we have to build up and for which we are responsible. It is surely easier to think that one can not help being what one is, than to know that one could be different if only one would endeavor earnestly enough.

This is probably the strongest reason for the approval the theory of heredity has met. This success is rather amazing. One would prefer to think that man would be glad of being given a chance to get rid of his bad habits and undesirable qualities, since so many people are profoundly dissatisfied with themselves and so little satisfactory to others. But no; people look askance at him who tells them that they may become different if they would only really try to do so. Striving for this goal, however, does not imply only exertion, long-lasting work, patience and courage; it implies also acknowledging really and wholeheartedly that one is in need of improvement. The one is contrary to the innate laziness of human nature, the other is offensive to vanity. Both tend to make man inclined to accept every theory affording a good excuse for not attempting any change and for just staying on as one is. To see this attitude justified by "science" is surely a great consolation.

PART II

ON TROUBLES, DIFFICULTIES AND FAULTS

1. Introductory Remarks

The more or less abstract discussions of the foregoing chapters would be almost useless if they could not be made to serve practical purposes. Practice without theoretical foundation is not worth much; it may be quite efficient for a time and within certain limits, but it is sure to come to a deadlock as soon as some new and unwonted problem arises. Chesterton was quite right in saying that in such a fix one does not need a practical, but an unpractical man, one who knows of the theoretical side of things; the practical man knowing only what used to be done, but not what can be done. On the other hand, theory which does not develop into practical application may be very interesting, but it is nothing to profit by in every-day life. Real help can be obtained only by a happy combination of both. To-day there is a tendency to overemphasize the practical side and to speak in a rather disparaging way of theory. This sort of mentality is a real nuisance; it proves to be a serious obstacle to all progress. Theory may be, and often is, bloodless and it may appear to be a lifeless thing; but mere practice is no better; it is alive and near to things, but it is also narrow-minded and incapable of discovering new sides of reality.

This part of the book will deal with many of the troubles and difficulties besetting our life. It will try to unveil their true nature and thus prepare for a discussion of the ways and means to tackle them. It is, of course, not possible to give a full catalogue of all the various difficulties man encounters in life, not even of those which have their origin in mistakes and faults committed by man himself. The only thing to be done here is to pick out some characteristic and frequent types of misbehavior and of difficulties and to analyze them so far that the method becomes clear and applicable also to instances not mentioned in these pages.

There are two ways open for this discussion of practical problems and difficulties. One can try to classify them according to some general principle of psychology. This would do very well in a treatise on psychology or on character; but it would become tedious and give rise to unnecessary repetitions. It seems better to go the other way, that is, to start from a division of practical aims and to describe the difficulties handicapping the realization of these aims.

The aims, then, every man pursues may be grouped under four heads. They have to do either with social life, including the relations to the members of the family; or with work, which means not only the job one has, but all kinds of activity; or with perfection, which term signifies here moral perfection as well as every other kind, for example, in the line of general culture or of intellectuality; or lastly with religious progress.

This division is not what one would call a scientific one, since it does not draw sharp lines between the single groups. They indeed overlap on many points. Troubles of social behavior endanger oftener than not work, since work nearly always implies co-operation. Religious progress and moral perfection are evidently closely linked up with each other. Moral imperfection may become a serious handicap in social life. One and the same feature of behavior may influence achievement and progress in more than one of these four fields. Unpunctuality is as great a nuisance in regard to social relations as it is in connection with work. Lack of sincerity imperils religious progress very much; but it is also a grave moral imperfection and conditions quite often rather unpleasant social situations.

The division proposed here is nevertheless not an arbitrary one. It corresponds to well-defined classes of values or goals. But human personality is a whole and acts as such. No side of it can be isolated from the rest. The classification used here does, accordingly, not imply that there are sides of human personality independent of each other. But, on the other hand, there are faults or habits which become particularly manifest and troublesome in one of the four fields, even though they are not without influence for behavior in other respects. It seems a good way to describe the single features under the heading of the type of behavior where they are apt to become more troublesome and where they, accordingly, are most easily discovered.

2. *Difficulties in Social Life*

Social relations are not all of the same kind, though they are all based on the fact that man is a social animal and that the development of his moral and intellectual faculties depends on his getting in touch with and living with his own kind. The structure of society is, however, a very complicated one, today even more than it ever has been before. In primitive society there is no great differentiation of the relations established between its members. But notwithstanding the complexity of modern life the relations between the members of society have remained essentially the same. There is perhaps but one type of relationship which is missing in primitive society and which is very characteristic of modern times—the one between the employer and the employee. But even this is foreshadowed, as it were, in primitive society which in a relatively early state already knew the difference between master and servant. The complication of modern society is due not so much to the arising of new kinds of social relations as to the greater number of persons every individual is in touch with, directly or indirectly. There are, therefore, much more shades of the typical social relations. To become aware of this, one needs but look at the social structure characterized by "authority." In primitive society there are but the head of the tribe, eventually the priest, and the father to exercise authority. Nowadays we have all the different forms of civil and political administration, the authority of the "boss" and his underlings, of the teacher, and so on. The attitude against authority is therefore liable to show a great many varieties.

There is perhaps no factor more important in the development of modern life than what one may call the disappearance of distance. It is by this that modern man gets in touch with so many of his fellows with the result that his individual life comes to be influenced by facts which do not touch him immediately. The improvement of the means of communication has nearly abolished the feeling for distance. Today the idea of getting to the moon does not sound preposterous any more. Traveling round the world in eighty days was, to the mind of Jules Verne, as utopian as being shot out into the universe for landing on the moon. Today men make this trip around the world in eight or even in six days. Our grandfathers could easily ignore what was going on in China; trade suffered a little, it is true, but the political situation in Europe or in America was hardly influenced at all. It is different with us; wars and treaties in far-off Asia have become exceedingly important, not only for governments, but for each of us.

Former generations could, if they were so minded, leave foreign politics and even domestic administration to the men in charge of them; today politics of every kind have a direct influence on the life of the average citizen. The factors determining individual life have become much more numerous and interwoven than they had been less than a century ago; they are very difficult to unravel; their manifoldness makes modern life appear so much more complicated and gives the impression that the social relations of today are different from those of earlier periods. But human nature remains, in truth, the same at all times and in all places. It has not changed; its essential features are just the same as they were thousands of years ago.

The complication of modern life makes a thorough knowledge of human nature more necessary than it ever was. Because of the great number of relationships everyone is in and because of the nuances of social behavior which follow from this fact, we need a better control of our behavior. The chances of getting into trouble are many times greater today.

The fact, however, that the essential features of human nature have remained quite unchanged throughout the ages explains why the reasons of our difficulties and troubles are but few and rather simple. The basic tendencies are still the same; it is only the way of expressing them which has become different. We do not, as a rule, kill any more the person we dislike; but the feelings of dislike or of hate are exactly what they were, and so with love and all kinds of sentiment. If human nature were not the same in all individuals and at all times, we never could understand and appreciate the art of foreign countries or of bygone ages.

The basic attitudes of an individual become visible mostly in social behavior, because society is, so to say, the natural atmosphere wherein man breathes. It is,

64

however, an exaggeration to consider social life as the only important side of human activity. Man is more than a social being; he is a person, that is, a being absolutely peculiar and unique, and he has duties towards himself as well as towards his neighbors. It is true that all sides of man's nature, that moral perfection or religious faith or his attitude towards work influence his social behavior. But this does not prove that all these sides of human nature exist for the sake of society. In certain modern psychologies and philosophies there is a definite tendency to overrate the place social life holds in human life in general. But society being the *milieu* in which man mostly moves, the social behavior reveals very often a great deal of the basic attitudes and motivations.

Because of the manifold and mutual encroachments it is not possible to order the various mistakes and faults occurring in regard to social behavior according to some general principle. Just for the sake of disposing of the whole matter, the following analyses start with certain features which enter into play in many of the social relations and turn afterwards to more special instances.

Though there are many ways by which individuals get in touch with each other and by which social relations are established, there is none as important as speech. Greek wisdom, accordingly, defined man not only as a social animal, but also as the animal gifted with speech. Speech is meant to express the thoughts one has and to reveal the feelings moving one and the wishes prompting one's actions. There is indeed the possibility of lying. It has been said that man was given speech that he may hide his thoughts. But there is also the rather mysterious fact that we are able to "see" whether a person speaks the truth or not, or to "see" whether he is playing a rôle or showing himself as he really is. This fact proves that there is in human nature a faculty of directly glancing at personality, unaided by words. A man must be very clever indeed to play a rôle without being ever found out. But of these things something more will be remarked later.

Speech may be considered from two points of view. We can turn to the meaning conveyed by words—for instance when asking whether they are true or not—and we may pay attention to the merely formal side of them. Regarding the latter there are three phenomena which deserve to be mentioned: talking too much, exaggerated taciturnity, and indistinctness of enunciation. All three are often a great nuisance in social life, and all three are apt to make a bad impression.

A Chinese adage says: "Great will be the reward of the husbands of the talkative hereafter" (though it is not always the wife who does the talking; there are plenty of male chatterboxes too).

According to general opinion garrulity is just a bad habit springing from a certain kind of temperament, due to a lack of self-control or of inhibition. This is evidently quite true; but it is not a sufficient analysis of this habit. Many people know perfectly well that they are talking habitually too much and that they make, therefore, a bad impression or even get into trouble. They know that to refrain from this habit would be the right thing to do; but strive as they might, they relapse again and again. To refrain from doing something seems not so difficult; one imagines that not talking could be easily achieved. But the garrulous person will go on talking too much, will go on knowing that he ought to be silent more often, knowing also that he ought to get rid of this habit, and nevertheless giving up not the least bit of it. Such a person has many reasons for not talking and few, if any, for talking; but the reasons he has for refraining from talking are apparently not strong enough; there must be some hidden force driving him onwards and keeping up this habit of garrulity. There must be some very strong, though unknown, desire which is gratified by the empty and useless flow of words.

Since the mere function of speech cannot give any pleasure—it does so only during a short period in early childhood—the motives for garrulity must be sought for in its effects. The tenor of what such a person says has no noticeable effect, since all this talk is almost exclusively on trivialities. A garrulous person has but seldom something of interest to say; even if he has in store —as many of them indeed have—quite a number of more or less good jokes or anecdotes, he very soon becomes a bore because nobody likes to listen only to such things, or only to one talker, and because even a large store becomes sooner or later exhausted and then the stories begin to repeat themselves.

An overwhelming majority, however, of these untiring talkers know of no other subject but their own personality, their own experiences, their own ideas. But their personality is generally uninteresting, their experiences are shallow, their ideas lack all importance and originality. This talking about oneself is surely one of the motives of garrulity.

By applying the rules explained in the previous chapters one will be quick to discover another element in garrulity. So long as one person talks, no other can put in a word. An uninterrupted flow of words is a very efficient means for staying in the foreground and for imposing one's will on others. Garrulity springs indeed in many instances from conceit and from the will to play a prominent rôle. It is due not so much to a lack of inhibitory power or to a too vivacious temperament as to a longing for superiority.

A special variety of garrulity is the habit some people have of interrupting others and to break in into a conversation just going on; their remarks are generally not to the point. They are made either because the topic of discussion is not to the liking of such an individual, or because he cannot bear to be silent for a longer time. As a mere listener he is not noticed; and not to be on the stage even for a short time is insupportable to him.

Sometimes people will break in into a conversation simply because they feel bored by it; they do not care whether others are interested or not. They act as if they were entitled to be amused or interested. Whether their interests are shared by the rest of the company or not, is of no importance to them. They forget that the rights of another are at least as good as their own. But they forget also—and they are not the only ones to forget this—that subjective interest and personal liking are no criterion of objective value.

The longing for prominence and superiority at work in the mind of the garrulous is rather obvious. But it may seem paradoxical to state that the opposite behavior of taciturnity is the effect, or at least may be, of the very same factors. The arising of apparently contradictory features of behavior from the same reason is quite frequent. It will be, therefore, useful to demonstrate this once and for all.

Taciturnity, or the habit of keeping silent, of answering questions but briefly or not at all, of never volunteering information, is not so common as is garrulity. In some rare cases it is due simply to a lack of training; a man living apart from his fellows, being very much alone, may lose more or less the habit of speech. It is different with people who are daily in touch with others. The taciturn person is silent in the midst of others who are not. Taciturnity is not so great a nuisance in social life as is garrulity; he who does not utter a word risks less of becoming a bore than does one who talks too much. But he might become as noticeable by his silence as does the other by his chattering; such a silent person gives the impression of aloofness, of thinking himself superior to his surroundings and becomes by this, so to say, a strange body in the organism of society and acts therefore as an irritant.

Taciturnity must not be confused with modesty keeping silent in presence of one's betters. A student following silently, without thinking of putting even a word in, a discussion among known scholars is modest, but he is not taciturn. Taciturnity shows in a reticence to speak on occasions when an average man would not hesitate to do so and when tact and duty ought to compel everyone to speak.

There is an absolute and a relative taciturnity. The first acts, as it were, on the principle of avoiding utterances as far as possible. The second becomes manifest only under certain circumstances; some people know but one subject to talk upon, for instance, their own job or hobby, and they become taciturn whenever they feel the audience not to be sympathetic. There is, furthermore, the taciturnity of the man who despises small talk and opens his mouth only to proffer solemn and serious statements. Such a man is usually devoid of all sense of humor, a quality much more lovable and even more moral than it is generally considered to be. Humor indeed is based on a sense of detachment from one's own personality, a knowledge that the ego and its petty affairs are not so important after all.

Taciturnity is due not to a physiological inhibition of the language-function; it is the effect of a definite inner attitude. A taciturn person may learn to behave in a more normal manner. He generally does so easier than the garrulous learns to refrain from chattering.

Taciturnity is often taken as a sign of a deep mind and as coupled with seriousness. But is rather often but a veil which in fact conceals nothing at all but conceit and shallowness. It may be the behavior due to a generally depressed mind which has lost the faculty of appreciating things; cheerful people are usually not given to taciturnity. It may be the effect of bashfulness and embarrassment.

In some cases it is quite natural to feel embarrassed; either one finds oneself in a really "embarrassing" situation, or one has to face a man commanding respect. But even then, embarrassment is not as inevitable as people will have it to be; one may be very modest and very conscious of another's superiority without resorting to the typical behavior of embarrassment. Mostly, however, embarrassment arises in situations which do not warrant such a reaction; the really embarrassed man finds himself in this mood always, even though he knows quite well that there is no reason for feeling this way.

Some time ago a young girl was supposed to be bashful and demure; today this kind of behavior is no longer appreciated. Neither girl nor boy wants to be bashful. The habit is nevertheless still quit frequent, and it is considered a definite nuisance. People affected this way would gladly get rid of this habit; but they believe this to be impossible, bashfulness being, as they think, none of their doing. They accuse their lack of social training, mistakes made in education, an unhappy temperament; they do not doubt that their bashfulness is quite independent of their will and their personality.

Bashfulness usually disappears after the person has become accustomed to the situation provoking this reaction; a bashful person has to feel "at home" in order to behave in a normal way, or to know that he is welcome to the other members of a set. The fear of not being welcome is indeed at the bottom of bashfulness and embarrassment. Were a bashful individual sure of making a good impression and of being received, as it were, with open arms, he would not behave as he does. He is, in fact, greedy for social success and not sure of attaining it. Sometimes this becomes very apparent from the comments such a person makes on his behavior and on the awkward impression he creates; he is convinced that he would make quite an impression and be liked by all people, were it not for his bashfulness. This quality is indeed accepted as a good excuse not only by the bashful person himself, but also by others; clumsy behavior, mistakes, even some impudence are overlooked because they are attributed to bashfulness. Bashfulness succeeds in having its owner taken at his valuation; he manages to persuade others that he really is quite nice and that this niceness is only dimmed by his unlucky habit.

This habit has but little, if anything, in common with true modesty. It is aping modesty, even overdoing it, but it does not spring from it. True modesty avoids doing whatever may cause conspicuousness; but embarrassment and bashfulness make a man unduly conspicuous. They do still more; they represent a definite appeal to the benevolence of other people. It is as if the bashful person said: "I am so bashful, so poor, so helpless, that you really have to be very nice to me." True modesty is natural and unsophisticated; bashfulness is not. A modest man will stay in the background in an unobtrusive way, and he will come forward if necessary; the embarrassed and bashful person contrives to stay in the background so that everyone becomes aware of it, and he will, when asked to step forward, protest so much that he becomes still more noticeable. There are many people who want to be noticed at whatever price; they are ready to be considered foolish and clumsy and what not, if only they do not pass unnoticed. The close relation between bashfulness and taciturnity is easily discovered by taking account of the remarks made just before.

Bashful people often speak very indistinctly; the emotional state they are in gives rise to some trouble of articulation. This habit is quite helpful, in a way; the bashful or embarrassed person fears he could say something wrong and create a bad impression; if he is difficult to understand he may still give another meaning to his words. But there is another kind of indistinct speech too, which occurs independently of embarrassment. It generally denotes a lack of consideration; the listener has to strain his attention for finding out what his interlocutor says; the latter not taking the trouble of expressing himself clearly. A certain habit of muttering and blurred speech springs from the same reasons. Indistinctness of articulation is often a kind of compromise between taciturnity and the necessity of social contact.

It is known that embarrassment may condition quite a flow of words; there is a stammering and a chattering variety. The embarrassed is however handicapped by his consciousness of himself and by his wish to make an impression; he is, accordingly, not able to think of a somehow interesting topic. But one topic exists which is always on hand: discussing one's neighbor. This kind of empty prattle is called gossip.

Gossips are a great nuisance, in more than one sense. By listening to them one gets the impression that there is nothing in the whole world to be talked of but what Mrs. Smith did, and how Mrs. Jones behaved, and that Jack was seen with Jane. Another type of gossip is very eager to dig out all kinds of political trash; he knows for sure that Senator X did this and that Mayor Z intends to do that. Gossip may be harmless, but it verges quite often on calumny and causes serious damage. This is generally known, even to some of those who indulge in this pleasant habit. Though they are aware of this danger, and though they got perhaps already in trouble through it, they seem quite unable to leave it; it is so lovely a pastime and exercises so great a fascination that they will do it over and over again. It is indeed not easy to cease gossiping all of a sudden. A gossip is seldom alone; usually he belongs to a whole set cultivating this amusing game. The gossip feels he would be out of tune if he would not do as the others do. If he does not take part any more, he is sure to be dropped sooner or later. So he has to go on. And what else can one talk about to these people, he asks; they are not interested in anything, they do not want to hear anything but gossip; it were inconsiderate and fruitless to introduce another topic.

All this is but a more or less well-made excuse for a habit the gossip often feels himself to be wrong. And it does not explain the peculiar pleasure he gets from his conduct.

The characteristic words by which the gossip begins his tale are: Have you heard? Do you know? These people have always "tremendous and very interesting news" to tell; and it is always a "deep secret" they are imparting to each other, though there is no doubt that this secret will not be kept and that the "strict confidence" will be betrayed, and that the person enjoining it knows this beforehand. This enjoining of secrecy is a mere formula; it is the sacred rite to be observed by the members of the "Most Loyal Order of the Gossips." Everybody knows this "in strict confidence" to be an empty, though time-honored phrase; it has conscientiously to be preserved, because the pretence of secrecy is part of the fun.

Some people do know indeed how to keep a secret. But many have still to learn it. It is not a habit natural to man; he does not feel well in having to conceal something. Children knowing a secret will look mysterious and behave in a manner revealing clearer than words that they know it; they will gambol around, shouting: "I know something, I know something." They manifestly enjoy this knowledge; but it is only the already more or less sophisticated who are content with knowing; generally they find satisfaction only in telling the secret. They indeed want to tell it, but they do not like being found out. A child will love your making guesses at his secret as long as these guesses are wrong; but he will be very disappointed if by chance you guess right.

Knowing a secret and divulging it, because the other children or the adults can not guess it, gives the child a very definite sense of superiority. With adults it is quite the same thing. History tells of many an instance where the possession of some secret was equivalent to power; blackmail is based on the same fact. The phrase "in possession of a secret" reveals this circumstance as representing a definite value. Possessing a value increases the value of the one who has got hold of the thing. It is so with wealth or station or knowledge; it is so with secrets too.

This feeling of increased value, caused by the possession of a secret, is one of the motives of gossiping, but it is not the only one. It is but a truism to state that the "news" of a gossip deals mostly with things disadvantageous to someone. Gossips but seldom discuss deeds of valor or of kindness, nor are they generally interested in another man's good sides. If such things are mentioned by chance, the gossip will immediately suspect that there must be "something behind it."

Human nature derives a very marked satisfaction from pointing out deficiencies or from remarking on bad features of character and on moral faults, or from discussing failures and even misfortunes. This kind of conversation evidently supplies pleasant feelings of a quite peculiar quality. Man is, on the average, quicker in discovering his neighbor's deficiencies than in acknowledging his assets; quicker in seeing things he can disapprove of than in becoming aware of those he ought to admire. Objectively taken, this discovery of the unpleasant side of human nature is rather disconcerting. Defects as such are never pleasant to look at; a healthy person is definitely more pleasant than a sick one, a sane man is much more pleasant than one affected by mental disease. Looking at a healthy person, be it the health of the body or of the mind or of morals, ought therefore to make a much more pleasant impression than considering the opposite types. But there is, in many minds, a strange inclination towards the unhealthy and the dark side of human nature. It is not possible here to inquire into the reasons of this interest. But it is evident that by making sure of one's neighbor's bad qualities one feels definitely superior oneself.

Gossip is closely related to the habit of criticism. The profit gained by criticizing one's neighbors was once very aptly described by a boy of some fifteen years. "That's quite simple," said he; "by criticizing others I raise my own standard."

We are, all of us, something or even much of a pharisee. We all like to think that we are better than the rest, that we lack this bad quality we observe in Mr. A and that other we notice in Mrs. B. If this idea were true, we would be right in enjoying our being better, if we did attribute this to the grace of God and if we did thank Him for being preserved from this one fault. But we generally do feel less grateful to Providence than proud of our righteousness, as if this were due exclusively to our own goodness. It were well if we devoted some thought to all the bad things we would have done and are still capable of doing, only that circumstances and Providence kept us from perpetrating them.

Even a man who is thoroughly contented with himself and proud of his high moral standard, does not ignore altogether that he in truth is as capable of doing wrong as the very people he despises because of their depravation. There is, in the depths of the ego, a knowledge of its essential imperfections. But pride and vanity do not allow this knowledge to develop. It would be too disturbing if we became fully conscious of our imperfections; it is much better to look away from them and to turn to those of others. By this we get the consolation that they are not better than we are, that they are even worse, and that, therefore, we need not reproach ourselves for not having reached a higher level of morality. This is the strongest reason for the pleasure man derives from detraction and gossip.

A peculiar variety of this habit consists in a kind of strict moral criticism masked in a care for the moral welfare of others or of society. Certain people feel themselves to be guardians of public morals and believe it to be their duty to expose all immorality. It is told that a certain lady complimented Doctor Johnson on his famous dictionary, remarking: "I am so glad, Doctor, that you left out all impure words." The doctor replied: "Did you look for them?" The idea of having to defend public morality affords quite a good pretext to certain gossips.

Others know still other reasons for indulging in the habit of criticism. They have to be on the lookout for the bad qualities in their fellows because they needs must know them for the sake of business, or because they want to have intercourse only with people of an unimpeachable morality. They are sure that all men are egoists, thinking but of their own advantages, trying to cheat and to embezzle everyone who is stupid enough to believe in good intentions, in love of truth, in kindness or in reliability. Caution and distrust are, however, not identical. Making use of a legitimate caution does not mean developing an attitude of general distrust. These critics spoken of here do not, as a rule, limit their criticism to those cases where to be cautious is all right; it becomes with them a general habit, and that is the point where it becomes utterly wrong. There is, in the world, definitely more of criticism than of praise, more of detraction than of appreciation. Man finds greater pleasure in tearing down his neighbor and looking down on him than in admiring him and looking up to him.

It were a sign of foolishness should one advocate a blind trust in everyone; caution has to be used, especially when there are some greater interests to be considered. But it is wrong to make this a rule for our behavior against your neighbors.

Critical people are not loved; they may be quite amusing if their remarks show some spirit, but they are not loved. Nobody feels sure that he may not be the next target. These critical people sometimes wonder at their not being favorites with their fellows. There is no reason to wonder. Even without a deeper psychological analysis their neighbors feel that the habit of criticism springs from an engrained egoism. The critic does not love his neighbor, and so he gets no love in return.

There are several ways of uttering criticisms. The critic may assume the attitude of the objective observer, of a naturalist describing the animals inhabiting some foreign country. He may behave as the expert in human weakness; he may be bitter or ironical; he may play the good-humored sceptic. An analysis of the different moods conditioning the single attitudes would lead too far. Only one of them has to be mentioned at some length, because it gives rise to serious difficulties, notwithstanding its appearing rather harmless. This is irony.

Ironical people are generally disliked. They are amazed at that, because they do not see anything wrong in their way of dealing with their fellows. Irony, however, is universally resented. It sometimes, indeed, has its place; we may make use of it to demonstrate the nonsensicality of an opinion, or for refuting an adversary in debate. But a behavior which is quite right under certain conditions may become wrong when generalized. Only the absolute moral attitudes, like love, are right always and everywhere. What is not absolutely right or good has but a very restricted field of appliance, and what is definitely bad has none at all.

Irony, like criticism, to which it shows kinship, springs from a conviction of, or a striving for superiority. It uses the sharpness of wit and often a considerable amount of intelligence to make light of things which others take seriously or which they admire or which they love; irony seems to point out to others that they are wasting their feelings on things not worth while. What is taken seriously is, in the eyes of the ironical, mere foolishness; what is admired is mere triviality; what seems great is petty; enthusiasm is based on illusions; love is but a happy mistake. People do not like at all this destruction of their ideals. They do perhaps resent it not because of absolutely pure motives. In remonstrating against sceptical irony, they defend not so much an ideal because it is such, but because it is their ideal; that is to say, they resent irony because it doubts their capacity of discerning what is great and true and good. Irony indeed directs its attacks only apparently against the ideals; in truth it attacks the idealist. It is but another method of enabling man to look down on his fellows. Of all behaviors, irony has to be used with discretion.

Irony is but one way among many others to express that one "knows better." The ironic and sceptic people "know better" only in a negative way; they know, or rather believe they know, that things are not as valuable, not as tragic, not as great, not as true as the average man will have them. Irony and scepticism, though they very often become a real nuisance and do anything but help their owner along, are after all supportable when they are associated with a good deal of humor. But the man who "knows better," who is always right, who believes himself entitled to bestow his advice and his wisdom on everyone and on every occasion, is deadly in earnest and utterly devoid of humor. He is one of the most unpleasant social phenomena.

Nobody can be right always; nobody can "know better" on all things and in all situations. It is much already when a man knows thoroughly one thing; the more he knows the more he will become convinced of not knowing all. The specialization of every kind of knowledge, its being split off in numerous small chapters, each of them long enough to fill a man's life, this whole development of newer times has made it impossible to one man—unless he be an exceptional genius —to accumulate real and thorough knowledge on more than one or, at the best, some few restricted topics. It is generally the man who knows nothing thoroughly who pretends to "know better" on any matter. He may have specialized on some topic and be really an authority there; but this does not make him an authority on other things as well. The "know-betters" do not, as a rule, belong to the class of the specialists.

There are some jobs which, unluckily, tend to make knowing better a habit. They need not do so, but they do very often. If a man has officially, so to say, to know better for some hours every day, he will easily assume this attitude for ever. Some specialists develop this unpleasant habit because they have to be an authority so often and to so many people that they retain this attitude also outside the shop. The specialization of modern working life, however, makes it more urgent than it ever has been that a man leave his "shop-habits" behind when he turns his back on the shop. He ought to do so for two reasons. First, his forgetting about these things contributes very definitely to relaxation and therefore makes him fitter for his work when he resumes it the next day. Second, a mind which is revolving always around the same kind of problems is bound to become monotonous, a bore for others, and in danger of withering gradually or of drying up. The problems of the shop ought to be left behind; much more, of course, the habits.

The development of a habit is not a mere mechanical process; even for a habit to become established some kind of consent of the person is necessary. This consent may simply consist in a non-resistance; but whether taking the form of an actual assent, or a mere letting things go, it is always an act of will. A habit already developed is not at all beyond the control of will. It is not necessary to transplant, as it were, habits from the place where they may be more or less right and useful, to other places where they are not desirable.

A striking instance of the "know-better" type is observed quite frequently in teachers. A certain type of them goes on teaching also outside the classroom. People of this kind are incredibly boring, presumptuous, conceited and disagreeable.

A peculiar type is represented by the man who gathers all kinds of demi-knowledge from newspapers, encyclopedias and "popular" literature. The latter is indeed an inevitable nuisance. It is inevitable because man can not be denied the right to know and because things have to be presented to those not acquainted with the matter and lacking the necessary previous instruction, in a fashion that they may understand. It is a nuisance because this kind of knowledge cannot be but superficial and even partly wrong. One sometimes doubts whether ignorance, pure and simple, is not to be preferred to this half-knowledge imparted by "popular" literature. At least one would wish that the average man became aware of the incompleteness of knowledge gathered from these sources. Many indeed are aware of this fact and will gladly turn to one who really knows for further information. But there is one type, already mentioned, who relies absolutely on the knowledge he owes to this kind of literature. There are moreover certain fields of knowledge of which everyone believes he knows something. It seems as if people had the idea that they are gifted with an innate knowledge on certain things and need not trouble to learn something about them. Medicine is one of these fields; education is another.

The "know-better" habit is due to an exaggerated sense of one's own importance. By assuming the behavior of one who really knows better, a man expresses his feeling of superiority, though he may not be quite conscious of this.

Conceit and egoism and the desire of staying in the foreground are also at the bottom of another behavior which is very much resented by other people and makes them avoid the person addicted to this habit. There are persons who become quite intolerable by always harking back to one favorite topic regardless of the question, whether the rest of the company is interested therein or not. Very often the talk of such a man is about himself, about his achievements, his successes in business or with the rod or in golf. If he is more pessimistic-minded, it will be on his misfortunes, on the way other people treat him, on the petty troubles he has to wrestle with, on the unpunctuality of his wife or the unreliability of his secretary. When lacking in discretion and when meeting an audience willing to listen to such talk, he will boast of his "success" with women.

A variety of this type is what one may call the "special reporter of catastrophes." The very moment such a man has got hold of some painful or troubling news, he will rush to the telephone and call up the person who probably will be most shocked by this news. This type is not necessarily of a pessimistic mood; he may be quite a cheerful kind of person. He enjoys very much this spreading of bad news. He revels so much in spreading the news that he does not care whom he tells it to. The young wife of his neighbor dies; he has seen her but once or twice; he hardly knows the widower; but he will go and tell whomever he meets: "A terrible disaster. . . ."

The "reporter of catastrophes" is often not content with repeating all tales on misfortunes he can get hold of; sometimes he goes so far as to invent some or, at least, to predict them.

The motive for this behavior must be sought for in the wish of playing a rôle, of staying in the middle of the stage; another important factor is that such a man makes use, for his own ends, of the aforementioned strange passion for the uncanny, the cruel, the horrible, the ghastly, lurid, terrifying things. The crowds which in the times of old pressed around the scaffolds did not assemble to see justice done and the criminal punished; though this idea may have been faintly alive in some of them; they thronged there because they foresaw the peculiar pleasure this spectacle was to give them. It is the same feeling of an uncanny curiosity which today causes so many people to try to get a glimpse at a man

run down by an automobile or to go out of their way
when they hear of some disaster a few blocks farther on.

The feelings which prompted and still prompt man
on these occasions have nothing in common with the
lofty sentiments of "fear and pity" which according to
Aristotle are the effect of witnessing a tragedy played
on the stage.   Nor are these catastrophes necessarily
pure tragedies, though they are usually called by this
name.   There may be a tragic element in certain disasters; but generally it is a misuse of this name to call
tragic a railway crash or an inundation destroying a
village.   These facts are horrible, very sad, but they
lack the essential characteristics of tragedy.   Tragedy,
whether conceived by the mind of a playwright or occurring in reality, implies guilt.   The tragic hero is a
man who involuntarily and unavoidably becomes
guilty and who, by his tragic end, pays the penalty for
his guilt.   It were better to discard the term of tragedy
and to reserve it for the few cases to which it really
applies; the wrecking of the Titanic, for instance, was
a terrible catastrophe, but no tragedy in the true sense
of the word.

Such a restriction of the attribute of tragedy is desirable not only because one ought to make a correct use
of words, but also because thus the pleasure derived
from witnessing and discussing catastrophes would be
put where it belongs.   By calling all disasters tragedies
this pleasure becomes invested with a loftiness to which
it is not entitled at all.   The "reporter of catastrophes"
seeks not for the exalted sentiments of tragedy; his is
quite another mentality.   Nor is he pointing at the in-
stability of things terrestrial or moralizing on it, unless
it be in a quite incidental and superficial manner.   He is
not even satisfied with the pleasure the spectators of
catastrophes feel.   What he really wants is to make

others feel either this pleasure or, preferably, make them shudder and recoil.

One reason for this behavior is the fact that by imparting such news he is sure to command the attention of his audience; another that he thus moves their minds according to his will; he is, so to say, playing on them as on an instrument. Both results are gratifying to his will for power. A third reason which is at work in him and in his audience, is the longing for sensational experiences. Exceptional and moving facts are more easily found in the field of the horrible, the sad or the disastrous than anywhere else.

Average life is poor in sensations. The longing for excitement, however, is a common feature of human nature. It is justified up to a certain degree, since monotony is indeed depressing and apt to paralyze vital energy. But the greed for sensation and excitement often becomes more or less a danger. More people than one would imagine get into trouble only because of their desire for excitement. The prying into another's private life, the curiosity wanting to get hold of every secret, the tendency to tease or even to offend are partly due to this inclination. Indiscreet behavior of all kinds may spring from the same root.

Discretion and tact are two qualities indispensable in social life. They do not depend on culture or intellectual development; both are found to be present very often in simple and uninstructed people and to be missing in others having had a careful education. These qualities are partly due to innate disposition; they are, however, much more dependent on environmental influences, and most of all on the inner attitudes of the person. Both arise from the will to consider another man's feelings, rights and personal peculiarities. The lack of tact and of discretion—taking this word in its original sense of power of discerning—results from an undue concentration on the ego which bars the outlook on the personality of our fellows.

Mention has been made incidentally of the somewhat mysterious faculty with which man is endowed, of "seeing" another's personality even though he may try to hide it. This faculty is well-developed in children; it becomes less sharp in adults. One of the reasons taking the edge from it is the growing concentration on the ego. It is true that a certain egoism may give rise to a clearer sight of certain human qualities; but it discovers only such features as are immediately related to egoistic ends. The egoist, at least of a certain type, is often rather sharp-sighted for the bad qualities in his fellows, especially for those possibly endangering his own ends, but he is blind to their good qualities, unless they may be used for these same ends.

There is a well-meaning tactlessness too. Many people become definitely unpleasant because of the interest they take in the affairs of their neighbors, even though they may do so out of a wish to help. But not everyone we believe to be in need of assistance wants to be helped. Our actions on behalf of our neighbors have to be regulated in the first place not on the ideas we form, but on the wants they feel.

It is a very common error to believe that discretion and tact and consideration are qualities which enter into play only when we have to deal with strangers or, at least, with people not belonging to the intimate circle of our lives. One observes very often that a person using quite an amount of tact in his relations with strangers is absolutely devoid of this quality when he deals with the members of his own family. The nearer, however, someone stays to us, the more is he entitled to consideration and to discretion.

The troubles of social adjustment become particularly grave within the family. Many people get on quite smoothly with strangers and not at all with their own family. It is obvious that a harmonious family life is one of the most basic necessities, and that a great deal of all the unhappiness existing in this world comes from disturbances of family life. The strained relations one observes so often between husband and wife, between parents and children, between brothers and sisters—not to mention other members of the "clan"—result, in large part, from the lack of mutual understanding, of consideration, and of tact.

Misunderstandings cannot be altogether excluded. No man is capable of seeing quite precisely the personality of another. But misunderstandings would not be so fateful, if there were not the idea that one has to be understood. No real harm is done by a misunderstanding, so long as the party misunderstood does not take this fact as a personal offence or as being bereft of what is due him. Many misunderstandings could be made harmless by simply explaining what the matter is. Instead of this, people will take offence and become gradually estranged from each other.

Many misunderstandings are due to ignorance. This is especially true of the relations between husband and wife. Men and women generally neglect the fact that definite differences in the mentality of the sexes exist. Theoretically, of course, everyone concedes the existence of these differences. Practically, however, most people act as if they expected a person of the other sex to feel exactly as they do themselves.

Much has been written on the "differential psychology of the sexes." There are extensive studies, based on questionnaires and on experimental research work. The results of science have, however, but little influence on actual life. The problems the average man has to wrestle with are, perhaps, not the same as those psychology generally investigates. Common sense and unprejudiced observation probably tell us more about these problems than the largest treatises on psychology.

It is not for these pages to describe exhaustively the characteristics of male and female mentality. Only some few points can be touched upon.

Many troubles in married life start with the reproach, outspoken or only felt, of: You do not love me any more, you do not love me enough. This reproach makes much of certain observations. The husband and the wife observe that their mate does not behave as they want him or her to do. This they take to be a sure sign of missing or declining love. Both forget, or rather never knew, that the behavior and the expression of love is not the same in the two sexes. Each of them, furthermore, forgets that his mate expects him, or her, to behave in a definite manner, and that love has first of all to consider the wishes of the beloved. These wishes may seem foolish to a person of the other sex; but love seeking not what is its own, ought to put up even with foolish wishes. One of the greatest mistakes people make in regard to married life is their overlooking the importance of small things. The small things are in fact important not only here; in great things man very often needs not decide at all, decision is forced on him. But in the small and apparently insignificant events of every day he needs character. Life, after all, consists just in a series of small events.

Men very often do not understand women; women are often incapable of understanding men. In truth the latter are still more gifted in this way than are the first. But women rather often do not care to make use of this faculty, because they feel it to be their right to be understood first. The idea of having to get first something before one will give, is one of the most disastrous mistakes man makes. But things may seem small to one and important to another. A witty Frenchman once remarked: "You may lay the whole world at the feet of a woman, and she is capable of refusing it, because the wrapping is not to her taste." The average man thinks wrappings of no importance at all; what is within alone matters. But a woman may feel that the wrapping is very important indeed; and she is not so wrong either. A gift is precious not only because of the real value of the thing given, but because of the loving care devoted to choosing and to presenting it. The salesman knows this, and he has, therefore, special "gift wrappings" on hand.

The stress laid by the female mind on certain details may appear very foolish to the average man; but it is an essential part of her nature, and one has to take account of it. There are, on the other hand, some peculiarities of the male mind which have to be considered, even though they may seem queer or foolish according to the female point of view.

Much trouble arises from an overexacting attitude assumed by both the husband as well as the wife. This attitude becomes troublesome not only in marital life, but in all kinds of family relations. It develops very often in persons who have, outside their home, to do with many people; they have, of course, to consider the peculiarities of those they deal with, because of the interests of business, or because they have to work with these people, and so on. They come home tired by having to consider others and by discovering over and over again that these people are not at all what one would want them to be. The people at home, at least, ought to be what one expects; they at least ought to be of a kind to make consideration and self-control unnecessary. But human personalities will have their peculiarities, even in one's wife and one's children. Nobody is entitled to expect other personalities to fit exactly his wishes. In a newly married couple each partner expects the other to conform to his own wishes and ideals. Each hopes that the other will change, neither is ready—at least in a great majority of marriages—to adjust himself. But if each persists in making demands and is unwilling to make concessions, the result is bound to be rather dreadful.

A very bad habit, which produces the worst consequences, is the one which spares all good manners for strangers and forgets them at home. A husband who forgets his manners as soon as he is at home can not expect his wife to be as tidy as he wants her to be; a woman who sits down unkempt and negligently dressed at the table, can not expect her husband to take care of the furniture. This looseness of manners becomes a great handicap in education too, since the children learn by this to disregard rules.

The husband lying down with his shoes on the bedcover does not mean to be aggressive; but his behavior is felt as an aggression by his wife, and it expresses to her that he does not value her work and that he neglects her wishes. Men very often are not sufficiently aware of the peculiar relation a woman may have to things. A man is careless about things, especially if he can easily afford to get new ones. But women, like children, have quite an attachment to the things they handle. The female attitude is, for that matter, indeed quite right; things are gifts, entrusted to our care, and by mistreating them we show a lack of reverence for God's creation.

The "know-better" attitude, sketched out above, becomes a special nuisance in family life. It assumes there often the form of infallibility. This becomes very dangerous in the relation between parents and children. Children cannot but discover that the parents are not always right and that they too make mistakes. By keeping up the pretence of infallibility, the parents run the risk of undermining their authority.

All these mistakes causing so much trouble in the life of a family spring lastly from egoism, from an exaggeration of individual importance, from an undue longing for superiority and, consequently, from a lack of true love.

3. *Difficulties with Work*

The analysis of the faults or habits handicapping work will again start best with a discussion of the formal side of work and from this proceed to the material aspects.

Nearly all work is woven, as it were, into social organization; it means mostly working for and with others or under them. Human behavior as related to work has, accordingly, to obey the very same general rules which regulate social life. The necessity of the close co-operation of many individuals is the reason why the time-schedule plays such a rôle in all kinds of work. Conforming to this schedule makes the essence of punctuality. Not conforming to it is the habit of the unpunctual.

Punctuality is not only, as the saying goes, the politeness of kings, and not only a necessity resulting from the organization of work and not only something whereby the "boss" may bring pressure to bear on his employees or the teacher on his pupils; it is in fact a moral quality. Unpunctuality is not just an unpleasant habit endangering work and eventually putting a man out of a job; it is rather a serious lack of moral perfection. This quality could, therefore, be mentioned also under the head of moral imperfection; but is best discussed here, because it becomes most apparent in regard to work.

The primary importance of punctuality is generally acknowledged. There is nonetheless quite a number of persons who go on being exceedingly unpunctual, though they risk losing their job, or of having a very disagreeable interview with the "boss," or being punished in some way, or being at least overwhelmed by reproaches and unfriendly comments from those they have kept waiting. These are not at all pleasant experiences; but they somehow seem to be not impressive enough to make an unpunctual person give up his habit.

He has, of course, a pretty collection of excuses on hand. The watch has been unexpectedly slow or stopped for some unaccountable reason; he overslept, having come home very late last night; the traffic was blocked; an unexpected call had to be answered; a paper he had to take with him had been mislaid; he did not feel well, etc. In some cases there may be indeed truth in all these statements, but generally there is none. And even if it is true that this man, for instance, did have to search for a letter, it is after all his fault that it was not ready for him to take it.

We speak of unpunctuality only then when a man is habitually late. Once in a while everybody may be late, though there are quite a few who manage never to be late even during many, many years. The habit of unpunctuality gives rise to many unpleasant experiences; there are not only those mentioned already, but the haste the unpunctual necessarily has to be in is itself quite disagreeable. The reasons for keeping up this habit must be very strong indeed, since all this unpleasantness is not weighty enough to counterbalance it.

The apparently invincible habit of unpunctuality has, as it seems, two main roots. The one is the reluctance against submitting to rules, the other is the idea of being able to cram a lot of things into a relatively short span of time.

Man is very definitely inclined to be disobedient. He does not, when left to the original impulses of his nature, feel like bowing to laws; he rather resents having to acknowledge them, and he will try to ignore or to break them whenever he can do so without incurring too great a risk. But his conscience tells him, notwithstanding this innate tendency for breaking the law, that there must be laws and that they have to be obeyed. Man may, in some exceptional cases, deny the existence of a law and of its obligatory power. Generally, however, the existence and compulsory nature of the law can not be gainsaid. Nor is there always a possibility of simply ignoring the law; circumstances will force man to recognize its existence.

The fact that laws exist and that human conscience is aware of this, is in absolute contradiction to man's wish for independence and to the impulses driving him into revolt and disobedience. He can not openly, not even before his own conscience, indulge in these inclinations. If he wants to gratify them he can do so only by some clever compromise, clever enough to become unintelligible even to himself. He has to find out some compromise between the inexorability of the law and his own longings. Such a compromise is found if some reason can be alleged for not obeying or at least not obeying completely, and if this reason can be made to appear as if it were independent of conscious will. This is exactly the case with the habit of unpunctuality; nobody is willingly unpunctual; even the most unpunctual individual has—or believes he has—the intention of being punctual. It is not he himself, not his conscious personality which makes him late; it is "his nature," something he can not help, an irresistible habit; or it is the strength of circumstances. Whichever reason is alleged does not matter so long as the unpunctual individual believes in the compulsory power of the factor he makes responsible.

Unpunctuality is, considered from this point of view, quite a clever compromise; it enables a man to disobey the laws of reality without feeling fully responsible for this truly nonsensical attitude. But there is still another side to this habit.

Sometimes one gets the impression that being late or unpunctual is not always as easy as one would think. There is the person who has to be at some place at a definite time; he knows very well that it will take him, say, half-an-hour to get there; he knows too—or rather he ought to know by experience—how long it takes him to get ready. To be at the appointed place in time he ought to begin getting ready fifty-five minutes before the time. He even begins in plenty of time; suddenly he has the idea that something has to be done before he leaves. This thing very often is not urgent at all; it could be done later in the day or tomorrow. But he starts doing it the very moment he ought to dress. He feels that there is time enough, though he indeed can not overlook the fact that there is not. Or he wants to finish the paper. There is, of course, some unpleasantness in having to leave anything unfinished; but sometimes we have to leave one thing for the sake of another, more important than the first. Or the man who has to get ready all of a sudden discovers that he wanted to look up a certain passage in Shakespeare for the past several days; now he comes to think of it, he just must go through some volumes, lest he forget again to ascertain the right quotation. Or he will simply do nothing, feeling sure that he is going to be ready in five minutes; but he needs in fact at least fifteen—and he knows that he does. This habit of interpolating something, of creating a quite unnecessary delay becomes particularily manifest in cases when such a person is reminded by another that he has to get ready. A husband is told by his wife that he ought to shave and dress; he answers, maybe with some impatience, "I know; just let me finish my cigar." Or a wife will, reminded in the same manner, reply: "Dear me, I forgot to ask Jane for the address of the plumber she recommended to me the day before yesterday;" and she proceeds to ring up Jane and becomes engaged in an endless conversation, perhaps not mentioning the plumber at all. They manage to lose quite a lot of time by such tricks; then they feel in a hurry, they try to rush things, but things do not like being rushed, and they take, as it were, their revenge by being obstinate and malicious. Buttons have a knack of becoming loose, keys of being undiscoverable, bootlaces of being rotten, cars of being unwilling to start, and so on, just when one most intensely desires all these things to go smoothly.

This behavior—which is quite common, though the picture drawn here may be something of a caricature—probably has no other meaning than to prepare an excuse for being late and to make possible just this being late. But why, everyone will ask, why should a person wish to be late? Well, there are many reasons for wanting to be late. Losing time and being unpunctual is quite an efficient method for making another angry who wants one to be on time, be it one who has to go with one, be it the person one is going to meet. Unpunctuality may serve for expressing a certain disregard for another or, at least, that one does not feel obliged to regard him too much. In former times it was a custom with the members of "society" to be late for concerts or for theater; in still earlier times the play could not begin before Lord this or the Duke of that had deigned to arrive. Even today there are quite a few occasions where the entrance of some great personality has to be awaited before the thing can be started. But the duke or the prince or the potentate used to be punctual, because they knew that the rest of the people would have to wait; they were punctual not so much because they did not want to keep others waiting, but because they knew for sure that nothing would begin before they appeared. They tried to be on time, for that made them conscious of their dominant rôle.

But there is still another factor, the one mentioned before—the tendency of cramming. The man acting in the way described above knows of course that there is a limit to speed and a limit to the number of things which can be done within a given number of minutes. But he acts as if he were capable of making time flow slower and of pressing things together. He acts as if the laws of time did not exist for him, rather as if it were he whom time had to obey.

Such an idea can not be conceived clearly and consciously; it is much too preposterous for that. It would be wrong if one were to impute to the unpunctual that they are thinking of ruling over time. But they act as if this were indeed what they think. There is another feature, coupled quite often to unpunctuality, the analysis of which brings out the very same idea. Many unpunctual people are exceedingly impatient. Impatience, of course, exists also independently of unpunctuality; but it is often the latter's companion. This is rather strange, because one would expect the unpunctual to show some indulgence for others having the same quality; but one will as a rule find them rather intolerant. In this they make indeed no exception; many people are quite severe on those who have the same faults as they themselves. Either they do not know their own faults at all, or they believe they have good excuses which are missing in the case of another, or they condemn others for not becoming aware of their being afflicted in the same way. Unpunctuality may, for that matter, foster the habit of impatience, because of the many situations necessitating haste and therefore creating impatience.

There are two kinds of impatience, one in doing things and one in letting them develop; they may be called also active and passive impatience. Some enlightenment on the nature of this quality may be gained by going back to the original meaning of the word. Patience is derived from the Latin verb *pati*, which signifies to suffer. The impatient person is one who finds it unsufferable that things do not behave as he wants them to, especially in reference to time. The passively impatient person feels it a torture that he has to wait. He simply "can not wait"; he will rather risk missing an interview than to have to wait for someone to see him. He is shocked and offended in finding that another patient is staying with the physician when he —he in person—comes to consult him. He suffers severe pains because the train is twenty minutes late, though he is in no hurry at all.

One can easily understand impatience in a man waiting for an important decision, for some news on which much depends, for a call from the hospital telling him that his wife is all right after an operation, and so on, though of course his being impatient does not make the world go faster. "Even the watched pot boils in time." One understands also the impatience of the child longing for his birthday-present, of the lover awaiting his beloved, of the author wanting to see his first book printed. We may understand, because we see the reasons for this behavior. But visible reasons are not necessarily good reasons. Impatience is, in fact, never reasonable. Active impatience is particularly not reasonable, because it tends to become an obstacle in realizing what the impatient person wants to see realized immediately.

In all the various shades of impatience there is one constant feature. The impatient person feels that he does not get his due. He believes that he has a right to expect the train to be on time, the physician to be ready to see him, things to behave as he wants them to. King Louis XIV of France, the same who coined the saying that punctuality is the politeness of the kings, once wanted one of his ministers to see him at three o'clock. The clock was still striking three when the minister advanced towards the king, who received him rather sternly, remarking: "My Lord, I narrowly missed having had to wait." When you go to see a king, you have to be in his ante-chamber a good while before the appointed time. The king has not to wait. Who chafes, because he has to wait, evidently believes himself entitled to kingly rights.

Active impatience springs from the idea that things have to obey. This becomes obvious in the behavior of children who want to punish things which do not behave. There was a king of Persia who had the sea whipped because it destroyed the bridges his soldiers had thrown across. This man believed himself a demi-god at least and felt outraged by the misdemeanor of the elements. But there are many adults whose behavior is not a bit better than that of children, though they can not pretend to believe themselves God-sent rulers over the world and the elements. They do but seldom punish things; but they do sometimes swear at them.

Impatience does not further our work, which usually progresses the slower the more impatient we become. This is true of single actions as well as of long-lasting enterprises. A man impatient to see the fruit of his work is liable to destroy it. Children will sometimes, having planted some seeds, dig them out every day to see how far they have progressed; there is but little chance that they will live to see the flowers. Adults often behave in the same manner. This kind of impatience amounts to an intolerance for supporting and watching any slow development, and it may be that it is the effect of discouragement.

A person trying to learn something, to acquire a new technique, to master certain difficulties, discovers that he is not progressing at all. He therefore begins to doubt whether he will be able to reach his goal; he is too ambitious, he cannot content himself with an average or medium success; he wants a great success and he wants it quickly. But reality does not, as a rule, concede such easy and quick victories. This man loses his patience; he begins to be hasty, and by this creates new obstacles. Finally he gives up; he will not say that he did not go on because he lost faith in his capacity for achieving his purpose; he will rather say that he is unluckily—by nature, of course—too impatient for this kind of work. Or he will complain that it makes him "nervous." The question of nervousness can not be discussed here; but one will always do well to remember that there are no sharp limits between nervousness and lack of self-control.

Another feature, rather related to impatience, is untidiness. Lack of order is sure to handicap one's work. But not all that impresses an observer as untidiness deserves really to be called by this name. The arrangement of notes and books on a writing-desk may appear as utterly untidy; so may the "disorder" reigning on the table of a chemist, or of a workman. But this disorder may have quite good reasons and be quite transparent to the man to whom those things belong. Order is not a category of aesthetics and it does not consist in symmetry or in a neat geometrical arrangement. Order means, at least in reference to work, that the things needed are handy, that they may be found at a moment's notice, that they are arranged according to the requirements of the work. Whether there is order or not is not shown by the mere aspect of the things, but by the way they help the work which they are destined to further.

Untidiness begins the very moment work becomes handicapped. The term "work" must be taken, however, in a very large sense; it comprises all kinds of dealing with things, not only in the office, or in the workshop, or in the kitchen; it refers also to the way a person dresses, how he arranges his daily life, his room, the way he answers his letters, and so forth. Whatever the special field may be, wherein untidiness becomes manifest, it always denotes an unwillingness to observe rules. Order means an arrangement according to certain laws; ignoring order amounts, therefore, to ignoring these laws.

Order, or the laws of which it is the outward expression, does not apply only to work in the strict sense of the term. A man may even be sufficiently orderly in his work and very untidy in other fields. There may be no grave inconvenience in being dressed in a disorderly way, as long as there is no violation of decency. But such a habit denotes—besides being unpleasant from the aesthetic point of view—a definite disregard of rules recognized by other people; this is tantamount to declaring that these rules do not exist for this one individual or that he is above the rules and above those who observe them. The story is told of Socrates who, meeting a very world-despising and very superior philosopher whose cloak showed many holes, remarked: "My friend, out of the holes of your cloak peers— vanity."

To each vice there is a corresponding virtue, since all evil is but the absence of the good. But among the virtues there are some which may be misunderstood and misused and distorted in such a way as to become nearly vices themselves. This is of course not a result of the particular nature of these virtues but of a behavior which—while keeping up the appearance of virtue—is in fact based on an attitude very different from the one demanded by virtue. The virtue corresponding to the vice or the imperfection of untidiness is orderliness and its exaggeration or perversion is called pedantry.

The behavior of the typical pedant is well known; no need to describe it. The pedant believes his habit to be a great help in work and in life in general; he believes also that it is a very moral quality and that he alone is the representative of true orderliness, whereas everybody else deserves more or less to be called untidy. Pedantry, however, very often causes a great loss of time and proves no help at all in work. The pedant, furthermore, devotes often such an amount of time to the preparations for his work—he is so exceedingly conscientious—that he never starts really working. He loses a lot of time in putting everything exactly in its place; but he could make quite often a better use of this time.

Pedantry complicates life, though it is intended to work the other way. Excessive pedantry is, however, more than just an obstacle in getting on with work; it is definitely an immoral attitude. The pedant tries to create around him a world arranged absolutely according to his ideas and subjected to immutable laws laid down by himself. This is in fact a petty manner of insuring superiority over things and, for that matter, over people too. Pedantry very often is a way of showing off one's own sense of order and giving others to understand that they are inferior. Pedantry may become also a very efficient means of tyrannizing other people; a pedantic husband or father or "boss" has many opportunities for avenging crimes, since nobody really can observe the laws of a pedant so exactly as to give him satisfaction. Even where he does not rule, the pedant finds a way of conveying to other people the impression that he alone knows what order means; he will come into a room and the first thing he does is to straighten out something or put a picture straight on the wall or shift the objects on the chimney-piece into an absolutely symmetric position.

Impatient and untidy people argue that their behavior is due to their "nature," that it is simply an essential feature of their character and that they can not, accordingly, help being what they are. The pedant feels that he has achieved a high degree of moral perfection, though he claims that he does but his duty and that he has to do this the more, since everybody else neglects it in such an awful manner. He alone knows what order really means, and he alone is sufficiently conscientious to act on this knowledge. An untidy person may possess quite a lot of charm, though his lack of order may be rather troublesome for many people and for himself too; but a pedant is not charming at all; he is simply a bore and a nuisance. He is sheltering himself behind his pharisaical attitude; his is in truth a peculiar type of hypocrisy.

Impatience, untidiness and pedantry are not restricted to work. They influence other sides of behavior as well. They could have been dealt with also under other headings; but they seemed to be best placed here, because they become most visible in connection with work.

The pedant is a person dreading new and unforeseen situations. He tries to arrange beforehand for every possible problem. By observing strictly the rule he has laid down himself the pedant builds around himself a wall which he hopes is going to exclude all events not accounted for. Pedantry tends towards a far-reaching simplification of life, shutting out as far as possible all sudden changes and replacing full-blooded reality by a shadowy and artificial routine. Pedantry is meant to warn against all situations such a man eventually would feel incapable of handling; it is a trick by which failure is to be avoided. Pedants are in truth cowards recoiling from the adventure of life.

The habit of circumstantiality is somehow related to pedantry. The pedant is circumstantial, but circumstantiality is not necessarily coupled to pedantry. Circumstantiality too tends to avoid action, by paying an undue attention to every smallest detail, by overrating the influence of merely accidental factors, by crediting with the greatest importance each single action, by discovering new difficulties at every turn of the way, by making a tremendous affair out of the most insignificant things. The overrating of details and of their own actions is the essential feature characteristic of persons cultivating this habit. Circumstantiality is a great handicap in work, because it slackens its progress; but it is also one of the greatest nuisances in social life; few people are as boring and as troublesome as the circumstantial.

The circumstantial person prides himself, like the pedant, on being particularly conscientious; he knows that every detail, even an apparently insignificant one, may eventually become important; his conscience does not allow him to overlook the smallest thing. These people are so conscientious that they have to ascertain whether some arrangement really suits everybody concerned with it; they will therefore go over each point with a minuteness which drives everyone else into despair. If the circumstantial person were really as considerate as he believes himself to be, he would not tax so much the patience of his neighbors; if he were really so much alive to the responsibility of human action, he would know that losing time is often a graver fault than neglecting some detail. These people do not know that shades and varieties of importance exist; they treat all things alike, as if they were all equally important. In truth they do not feel at all that things are important; what they feel to be important is exclusively their own doing. A thing has, in the eyes of the circumstantial type, no intrinsic value; no fact has an intrinsic importance; things and facts become valuable and important only because and insofar as this individual has to do with them. There is a strong element of egoism and subjectivism in this kind of behavior.

Neither untidiness nor pedantry nor circumstantiality are felt to be "abnormal"; they are considered as variations of normal character. There are other qualities imperiling work which, according to the idea of the subjects, verge on abnormality. It is very difficult to decide whether some character-trait belongs to normality or not. But this decision is, in truth, not of a very great importance, because there are fleeting transitions, not of course from normality to real mental disease, but from certain undesirable character features to others which create the impression of not belonging to personality but of being added to it, as it were, from the outside. Many people will deplore their being impatient, but they will—even though they may speak of this quality as a sign of "nervousness"—not consider this as a "symptom"; they will hardly seek the advice of a neurologist for the sake of getting rid of their impatience. But a person who feels that his work suffers by his "lack of concentration" is rather inclined to believe this quality to be the "symptom" of some serious trouble and to turn to the neurologist for help.

The fact worrying these people is too well-known to need a lengthy description. Some few examples will suffice to recall what is the matter with such a person.

A woman wanting to do some needlework finds herself suddenly awaking with a start, the work in her lap, her hands idle and her mind coming back from she does not know where. A boy, instead of doing his home-work, lets his thoughts wander away from his task and turns, while still sitting at his desk and perhaps still turning the pages of the book, to the last or maybe the next baseball game. A clerk going over some ac-counts finds that he has no idea of the figures his eyes are running over, because his mind is occupied with the memory of the last date he had with his girl or with pic-turing the pleasures of their next meeting. Those people are said to be "dreaming" instead of doing their work. They often know what they are dreaming of, but very often they have no idea whatever of the matter to which their thoughts turn. It is especially the second form of incapacity of concentration which is felt to be ab-normal. Sometimes one gets the impression that these dreams are breaking into the stream of waking thoughts and into actual occupations with an irresistible strength. A child or an adult may find himself sitting on his bed, his shirt in his hand; he seems to have forgotten alto-gether that he just was putting it on; something came between, he does not know what it was, and he glided off into some dream whose content he often can not even recall. Whether the distracting thoughts or dreams are known to the subject or not, the impression is regu-larly that this drifting away into the realm of dreams cannot be helped; try as he might, the subject can not get rid of this habit which he himself feels to be wrong and a very serious obstacle to his work.

Most of these people describe their state as if they suf-fered from a general incapacity for concentration. This is, in a great majority at least, an evident exaggera-tion. The boy who can not concentrate on his mathe-matics is very often quite able to concentrate on something else, for instance on building a canoe or on reading a thrilling story. The clerk whose thoughts wander away from his correspondence to dwell on his girl may forget her completely while following the races. The woman who drifts off into the land of dreams instead of mending her husband's shirts is able to concentrate perfectly when playing bridge.

It is indeed well known that concentration proves insufficient—unless it be an extreme case—only where there is no interest for the thing demanding attention. To concentrate on a matter which we feel to be boring or, even worse, tedious and disgusting is rather difficult, though it may be done and surely can be learned; but it is much easier to attend to things one is interested in. Another fact, belonging absolutely to normal mental life, which may serve to clarify the phenomenon of lack of concentration is likewise quite well known. If we have in mind some idea which worries us, some trouble or sorrow or a problem exercising a strong fascination, this thing will turn up again and again, without our wanting it to do so, even while we most earnestly try to give our whole attention to another matter. Attention is never of the same intensity during a long time; there are what is called by psychology fluctuations of attention. This phenomenon can be ascertained best by listening to the ticking of a watch; we get the impression that the noise becomes sometimes louder and sometimes quite low; the noise does not change in fact, but the intensity of our listening to it varies. These fluctuations of attention become intensified whenever there is something on our mind attracting attention.

The incapacity of concentration depends not so much on a deficiency of this particular faculty as on the presence of other things which attract our attention more than the thing we ought to concentrate on. This is a very typical instance of what is commonly called "weakness of will"; there is in truth no real weakness, but a partition of will or of interest, attention being distracted by some other topic, the term "distraction" having to be taken in its most literal sense.

The question is whither attention turns, rather than from what it is drawn off. If this is pointed out to people complaining of incapacity of concentration, they very readily accept this statement; but they add immediately that they cannot help being interested in other things more than in their respective tasks. Whether they can or can not help it, is another question. The first thing is to find out what the thing is which captivates their attention.

Sometimes it is indeed useful to become distracted. Says mother: "Dad, Bob needs a new suit. . . . But you don't listen to what I say!" Says father: "I just remembered that I have to contact Brown and Jones tomorrow about their last order." Why did this thought come to father just now? This very trivial fact shows that thinking of things which are not actual this moment may be an efficient way of escaping an unpleasant reality. Some people do not even want to escape totally; they only dislike to have to obey the summons immediately, they prefer to choose their own time.

The same tendency underlies the very common habit of postponing things. This habit may be so strong that a person addicted to it will risk even serious damage only for the sake of not having to do things immediately. A peculiar variety of this habit consists in resenting very much being told to do this or that. In some persons it becomes quite a habit of not doing what they are asked or told to do, simply to save their idea of independence.

The lack of concentration will be understood better in its psychological conditions by comparing it with another habit which has indeed much in common with the first: day-dreaming. The state of mind, indeed, which intervenes in work and causes the mind to wander is merely a more or less abortive day-dreaming. The day-dreamer may be a person who deliberately takes abode in a world of dreams and of unreality, not caring for real things and real tasks, or he may be one whose mind drifts away into this land unwillingly and without noticing it. Some of these dreamers do not know afterwards, where they have been; they only become aware of a lacuna, of quite a time having elapsed of which they are unable to give account. Day-dreams are, sometimes, as easily forgotten as are those appearing during sleep. But one can get a glimpse of the latter by awakening the dreamer suddenly; in the same manner one sometimes gets an idea of what is going on in the mind of the day-dreamer.

Day-dreams deal with things which are particularly dear to the dreamer's mind, things which attract him more than does reality. The world of the dream replaces all unpleasant sides of reality by features fashioned according to the dreamer's wishes. These wishes are fulfilled by the dream, either quite openly or in a more veiled manner. Day-dreams are always on the dreamer's own fate and personality; no day-dream pictures objective things; they are all about the dreamer's person and his doings. It is this feature which distinguishes day-dreaming from planning. He who has to figure out a line of action has to make use of his imagination; but his thoughts turn on reality, on what has to be done or can be done, and he starts therefore from the reality in hand. The dreamer discards reality more or less; he starts from some situation which interests or pleases him, and he does not care at all whether his dreams can become true or not.

The world of dreams has another quality too, besides correcting the unpleasantnesses of reality and picturing a "better world." The dreamer creates this whole world and it exists only by his will. He is, in fact, the almighty creator and ruler of this world. The dream therefore supplies a definite gratification to ambition; it satisfies the hidden but never-dying wish "to be like gods."

Day-dreaming is dangerous, not only because it removes the individual from reality and places him in a region where activity is quite impossible and where his ideas and decisions have no practical consequences, but also because it furthers the wrong and unruly ambition which is at the root of so many troubles.

Now, after having become acquainted with the true nature of the things which distract the human mind from reality and, accordingly from work, and which become the reason for the incapacity of concentration, one can try to answer the question, whether this habit is really, as the people addicted to it pretend, so utterly immutable. The considerations on this point apply, however, to some other habits too; it is therefore preferable to postpone the discussion of this point until later.

One may perhaps wonder at finding mentioned here, among the troubles regarding work, the fact of fatigue. Fatigue is apparently nothing the psychologist is entitled to discuss; it belongs to physiology or, eventually, to pathology; it depends on physical factors and has nothing to do with mental qualities. This opinion is, however, not quite correct.

There are people who get tired very quickly, so that they have to make great efforts for going on with their work. Others are capable of much greater exertions and of longer work without feeling tired. These differences are generally attributed to factors belonging to bodily health, or strength, or constitution. Fatigability may depend, it is quite true, on such factors; everybody knows that a man in a bad state of health gets tired more quickly than he does in his normal state. There are, however, facts which point to a definite influence of the mind too.

It is noteworthy that we use the term of "tiresome" nearly exclusively as a synonym for "boring." Being bored is no effort; it does not consume energy; none of the forces of our body is overtaxed by listening to a dull person, by reading an uninteresting book, by attending a tiresome meeting. Nevertheless we feel tired and sleepy. This proves that there is a feeling of being tired which is not conditioned by physical—or, for that matter, by mental—effort. The state of fatigue, resulting from an expense of energy has to be distinguished from the feeling of being tired. The latter may be caused by objective fatigue, but it may arise also independently. Fatigue may, on the other hand, exist without the feeling of being tired accompanying it; this is the case whenever emotional strain or the action of some drug—for instance, caffeine—overbalances the effect of exertion. The sportsman intent on securing a record, the scientist observing an interesting phenomenon, the mother watching at the bed of her sick child, the reader enthralled by a "mystery-story," the player sitting the better part of the night at the card-table— they all do not notice that they are really tired; their organism is in the state of fatigue, but the corresponding feeling does not arise.

Feeling tired is therefore no convincing proof of a real expense of energy, and getting easily tired does not necessarily show that there is a real weakness or inefficiency of the body. Physicians know of many cases in which the "patient" complains of his becoming tired very quickly and in which the most conscientious examination does not reveal any sign of physical weakness.

There is, furthermore, the fact of certain types of

people feeling exceedingly tired by one kind of work and quite capable of great physical exertions immediately afterwards. A boy may feel "too tired" to do his Latin, but not at all for playing tennis; a girl may be "exhausted" by her office work, but have strength enough left for dancing. Which again shows that the subjective state of feeling tired depends on still other factors besides the amount of work done.

Objective fatigue too is not conditioned by the amount of work alone; it depends, to a great extent; also on the way this work is done. There are many ways of doing the same thing; training consists largely in avoiding all superfluous movements and limiting muscular exertion to the absolutely necessary minimum. Lack of adaptation plays a great rôle in the causation of fatigue. We may speak of a mental adaptation too; it comprises emotional and volitional factors besides one of mere technique. The more one is willing to do a certain work the better he is mentally adapted to it. Really willing means to be wholeheartedly with one's work (even if one does not like it) because it is work, because it is the part allotted to one, because by doing it one joins the great army of working humanity. "Therefore I saw, that there is nothing better in this world, than that man be joyous in his work, for this is his part."

People who get easily tired by doing work which does not really unduly tax their forces are mostly badly adapted—in the sense alluded to—to their work, generally even to all kinds of work. They think that they like another work better and that they would be more efficient had they this given to them. Experience shows, however, that this is often not true at all. These people, when given other work, feel better at first; they do not feel so tired any more; but this state of things lasts but a short while; very soon they are as tired as they were before.

There are no doubt many unpleasant sides in many kinds of work. Pay may be—and very often is—insufficient; comrades may be rude and inconsiderate; the "boss" may be unjust and exacting; the work itself may be unsatisfactory for many reasons, and so on. One thing becomes a particular nuisance: work well done often meets no acknowledgment. A certain amount of recognition is due to man; to ask for it or to expect it is not vanity; the efforts of a man are not fully paid by the salary he receives, since there is more in work than its mere mechanical or outside aspect. The will to work, the readiness of filling one's place, all the mental factors coming in, demand a mental or moral compensation. Especially unpaid work, like that done by the housewife and mother, ought to be acknowledged; it is truly an injustice, this so frequent habit of husbands who take all the work done by their wives as a matter of course.

Not receiving one's due, not seeing one's work recognized is, on the other hand, no sufficient reason for abandoning it. Man would indeed not feel this way, were it not for the hidden but incessantly smouldering fire of revolt.

Even when we are best adapted to our work, quite willing to do it, this rebellion against having to do it may break out. One hears sometimes of strange facts; a man, successful in his work, honored for his achievements, who apparently has nothing at all to complain of, suddenly deserts his work, throws away fame and honor and success; he either retires, unaccountably, into solitude or, in some cases, disappears totally, nobody knows where. Such a line of action is open but to very few; most people can not and dare not give vent to their longing for desertion. But they can find some outlet for it. They can manage to degrade work by hating it and to feed their hate by feeling work too much for them, that is by getting tired.

Few people are ever really absorbed by their work or by any other occupation. The beautiful enthralment children show while playing is lost in later years. There is something left or revived of it on certain occasions which—rather noticeably—are all more or less called "play." The term "playing" is used for sportive plays as well as for those of the screen or the stage; we play at cards or roulette; a gambler is a player; and stories are, though we do not call them plays, at least "fiction"—make-believes—as every true play in childhood is. But work is no play. It is perhaps not so bad an attitude which looks at work as if it were some play; children are indeed at least as earnest in their plays as adults are, even the most solemn of them, in their work. But to enjoy one's work as if it were play is a very rare gift. And a dangerous one, because it but too easily degenerates into mere toying with work, which is quite another thing.

This may be, however; it is surely true that few people are really absorbed so deeply in whatever they do that their whole personality is, so to say, lost in their work. We are, all of us, mostly divided between our work and something else. This being divided is, even when it remains unnoticed, an unpleasant situation. The human mind has evidently a strong craving for unity and it dislikes being torn asunder. But man is never, or nearly never, so enthusiastic about anything that he can forget himself and his egoistic longings altogether. He is always divided between the objective reality and his own subjective world. Reality gets hold of him, he cannot escape it, he must give it attention. But the stronger he feels drawn towards his own subjective world, the more painful becomes this state of being divided. Man cannot put an end to it by throwing himself totally into reality and work, because the attraction the ego exercises is too strong. He can, therefore, end this situation of being divided only by returning into the egoistic world. But conscience forbids this; he cannot do it openly, he must find a way for doing it which will allow him to keep up appearances or, as the Chinese say, to save his face. That is, he must feel that he has a very good reason for deserting work and reality; this reason is supplied by his getting tired. This somehow paradoxical view has its confirmation in the fact that people in whose life the subjective world, the world of dreams and of desires, plays a greater rôle, are particularly liable to getting tired very easily: the neurotics.

It must be pointed out, however, that the diagnosis, so to say, is not for the layman; it can be made only after all possible reasons—and among them somatic factors—have been excluded. Sometimes a man accuses himself of being lazy and easily tired, while he is in truth suffering from some bodily ailment. Or schoolchildren are reproved and punished for being inattentive and distracted, while in truth their behavior is conditioned by some physical trouble, perhaps tuberculosis or some endocrinal disturbance.

This is, however, not the rule; generally people are quite healthy enough for the work they ought to do. If they feel not capable of doing it, or if they refuse to do it, the reason is probably not to be found in their physical state; most of them are simply lazy. Laziness is not always the same in everyone. Though its manifestations may be, or are, very much the same, the psychological background may differ considerably. The common idea is that all laziness is of a piece and that to trace it back to other reasons is quite unnecessary. There are, however, several reasons for being lazy. And it is accordingly wrong to suppose that laziness can be dealt with always in the same fashion. The idea that a lazy man has to do nothing but just to be not lazy, is wrong; one has to find out what the particular reasons for his laziness are.

A good many people are simply and always lazy; there is nothing to induce them to become industrious or even ordinarily active. They are as unwilling to undergo exertion in sports as they are disinclined to intellectual efforts. But there are others whose laziness is, so to say, more specialized. A boy may neglect his schoolwork out of laziness and be quite willing to devote much effort and time to training on the playground. But he may also be rather industrious in school and be too lazy for training. Thus far laziness is very much like fatigability; lazy people indeed very often complain of being tired. Laziness may cause an unwillingness to work, but the relation may also take the opposite turn.

Human nature comprises many apparently contradictory tendencies, which fact is indeed at the bottom of quite a number of conflicts. We feel drawn to idleness and, at the same time, dissatisfied when there is nothing to do. An old adage calls idleness the beginning of all vices. When man is not occupied by reality and not forced by it to obey its laws, he begins, as it seems, to invent occupations of his own which indeed easily miss the road of righteousness. There is a definite longing for activity in every normal mind; the aim of this longing is, however, not mere activity, but one which makes at least some fugitive impression on reality. Man wants to see his will creating things, and since he has no true creative power, the next best thing to do is to impart some change to reality already existing. On the other hand there is a marked repugnance against violent effort. What man really desires is to attain a great result by a small effort. This compromise is not feasible. A certain correspondence between effort and result seems to be one of the laws of reality. The solution of dividing the day into periods of work and of leisure is not altogether satisfactory, because the contradictory tendencies co-exist; while work gratifies the longing for activity, the tendency towards idleness is dissatisfied, and being idle leaves unfulfilled the wish for activity while gratifying the longing for idleness. The opposite tendency may be silenced for a while, but it does not cease to exist and it is quite capable of giving rise to some unpleasant sensations. The more a man is wrapped up in his work, the more the tendency of idleness is silenced; but it is never really destroyed. Ignoring it altogether may become even dangerous. This is observed in people who have developed an exaggerated habit of activity and suddenly suffer a breakdown; from overwork, it is said, but the true reason is often not the amount of work done but the disharmony created by the neglect of an essential feature of human nature.

The modern way does not allow for real idleness. People of today feel—at least in the towns and in places where city-civilization has become dominant—that they ought "to do" something even during their leisure hours. The capacity for being idle has been more or less lost; there is no place left any more for real relaxation, for allowing to vanish the unhealthy tension we have to live in the greater part of the day; modern mankind has therefore lost the capacity and the understanding of contemplation. Activity is all. Enjoying leisure, the *dolce far niente,* is unknown today. People ask each other, immediately after having left the office, the workshop, the classroom: "What are you going to do now?" This idea of doing has destroyed the faculty of conversation; a *salon* like those the eighteenth century, and even the nineteenth knew, is quite impossible today; nobody has the inner leisure to indulge in conversation for conversation's sake. Modern humanity is poisoned by restlessness. The dim feeling that something is wrong is one of the reasons why certain oriental philosophies find admirers, though the philosophy, as such, usually does not deserve this admiration. An equilibrium of activity and leisure is necessary; otherwise there is no chance of a man becoming aware of some fundamental truths about himself and the world. It is as wrong to lose oneself totally in the world of activity as it is to lose contact with it.

These remarks are not meant, of course, as a defence of laziness. Love and understanding of true leisure is not at all to be confused with laziness. True leisure is, in fact, possible only in contrast to and, so to say, on the background of activity.

Laziness may spring from a hidden rebellion against the law which compels man to work. Laziness is an efficient, though not a moral method for not obeying the rules of reality. A lazy man believes that he cannot help being lazy, that this quality belongs to the original make-up of his personality, and that it is, therefore, immutable. This conviction helps him in ignoring the true reasons for his behavior. In truth he is not shunning work as such, but rather the obligation it implies.

Lazy people do things, when they do them at all, often only half-way. They leave a part of them undone, they even take to cheating and to keeping up only the appearances. Such people often show quite a respectable amount of ingenuity in discovering ways of diminishing the burden of work. Mankind owes perhaps to laziness even some valuable discoveries; but this is not a reason for cultivating this quality.

Laziness may be the result of an overstrung and deeply buried ambition. A man who would feel satisfied only by very great achievements, but who doubts whether he ever could attain this goal, can not in fact do better than be exceedingly lazy. His laziness is the effect of a compromise between his fear of failure and his ambition. An allegory will make this point clearer: A man is possessed by the ambition to climb the highest peaks; but he does not feel equal to such feats. He is quite capable of scaling a mountain of moderate height; but this is, to his mind, the same as a failure, since it means resignation. Therefore he goes and settles in the midst of a wide open plain. And he says: "Would my home were in the mountains up North; I surely would climb Mount McKinley or one of those giants; but here, in the plains, there are no mountains, and I have neither the money nor the time for traveling so far." All this is quite reasonable; this man forgets but one detail: that it was by his own free will that he settled in the plain. The lazy man's talk runs in the same line: "What would I not do, if I were not so lazy."

Distrust in one's capacity, together with the wish for great success is very often at the bottom of laziness. Not so seldom this quality disappears when encouragement has set in and ambition has become less highstrung.

Laziness achieves but little. It has many reasons on hand for excusing its ways. One of these reasons alludes to a certain type of overactive and overenergetic people. The lazy man reproaches these people for overrating unduly the importance of work and of activity. He is of course quite wrong, and he knows that he is. But there is a certain type whose behavior apparently justifies the criticism the lazy makes so much of. There are people who can not be without doing something, but they too do things but half-way. They begin one thing and pass on to another, without finishing the first. They take up whatever crosses their way; today they are organizing something; tomorrow their whole mind is wrapped up with rearranging their collection of stamps; before having gone through the first third of it they turn to a new topic. They achieve not more, sometimes even less than does a lazy person. This is but another way of escaping from reality and its laws.

Overactivity is, as a rule, not due to a strongly developed sense of the amount of work to be done and of the objective importance of things; it rather springs from an overemphasizing the importance of doing. The accent is not on the work to be done, but on the doing of the work. To these people it is not of primary importance that this or that be achieved, but that they are occupied and feel that they are important and useful; in truth they are generally rather useless and but an encumbrance to those who really want to see things done.

The emphasis laid on the subjective side of activity tends to diminish efficiency. The attention we pay to how we do things is apt to deteriorate the quality of our work. The story of the centipede who was unable to move his legs since the malicious tortoise had asked him how he managed to know which of his hundred legs he had to move every time, is too well-known to be repeated here. It illustrates perfectly, however, the fact that our work does not profit at all, that it rather suffers, by the attention we pay to the subjective side of our doings. This undue attention makes us slower than we need be. There are indeed differences of what is called individual rate. These differences depend on constitution and temperament. But often there are other reasons, among which the factor of paying too much attention to our doing, instead of turning to what has to be done, is quite prominent. There is evidently a close relation between slowness and circumstantiality as mentioned above. Personal rate can be influenced by training. A hasty person may learn to slow down his actions. Acquiring a greater speed of action seems to be more difficult. An abnormally slow rate is sometimes due to special training and to education. There are parents who discourage fast action in their children, partly because the children have to be accustomed to attention and conscientiousness, or to caution for the sake of avoiding rash action, partly because the parents are over-anxious and fear that the child may hurt himself by running or by some other quick action. The same attitude may result from the idea of avoiding every mistake—which in fact is impossible—and of choosing the surest way. Pessimism and a distrust in one's own abilities as well as in reality in general are often associated with slowness.

Slowness may assume various forms. One person is slow during the whole series of single acts constituting some action. Another is slow to begin, though he may go on at a quite reasonable rate once he has started. A third will start at a more or less normal rate, but his actions will become gradually slower when nearing the end of his work. A boy may leave his home and move quite fast; the nearer he comes to the school—it is examination day—the slower he walks. He mounts the stairs haltingly. At the door of the classroom he comes to a standstill; it lasts quite a while until he turns the door-knob to enter. This dilatory policy is easy to understand. The behavior of this boy has many analogies in the life of adults. One has but to open one's eyes to discover them, in the behavior of others and of ourselves.

Slowness and hesitation mean loss of time—or a gain, if one looks at it from another point of view—and he who is but little minded to do a certain thing may profit by this attitude. He may linger until something comes between; he may tarry so long that the moment of action has passed. By these tricks he may escape doing what he does not like. Here again overstrung ambition may be of a decisive influence; by being slow one may well avoid failure, because slowness amounts to avoiding achievement. This is the price to be paid. He who wants to avoid all kinds of mistake, all kinds of risk, every failure, needs must end by doing nothing or by doing things in such a way that in truth nothing is done.

All the character-features described here are often not the result of a definite constitution or a certain type of temperament. They may be explained by very rational factors; they may be understood as the expression of definite attitudes, and they may become changed by changing these basic attitudes.

Different though these undesirable habits are, they all go back to one and the same root. They are all due to a disturbance of the true equilibrium between reality and the ego, objectivity and subjectivity. This is also finally the answer to the question as to what causes the lack of concentration, what makes up the content of day-dreams, and what is beneath such habits as impatience or pedantry or circumstantiality. It is always the ego which pushes, as it were, into the foreground, which attempts to occupy a place it is not entitled to; it is subjectivity trying to get the upper hand over reality. These attempts are bound to fail. Reality is stronger than the ego ever can hope to be. These attempts turn, moreover, against the ego itself; disregarding reality amounts to imperiling the ego too. But this will be considered in a later chapter.

The discussion on the difficulties related to work can not, however, be abandoned without just touching on one important question. Many people feel that they have been compelled—by fate, by circumstances, by the will of their parents, by chance or by their own once-cherished but nevertheless mistaken ideas—to choose a

job they do not like or one for which they do not have
the necessary qualifications and abilities. They are
thoroughly dissatisfied with their work; they dream of
having other things to do, and they imagine that they
would be much more efficient if they had a job according to their inclinations.

This question is very serious; it has, however, more
than one side. It is not sure, in the first place, that
inclination and ability are so strictly correlated that the
presence of the first may be considered as a reliable sign
of the second. One has but to think of the many people
who believe in their being gifted for some kind of art
—usually it is the theater or the screen, but it may be
painting or poetry too—and who are in truth but mod-
erately talented, if at all. There is, furthermore, the
fact that certain careers appeal in a peculiar manner to
certain periods of life; children and adolescents have a
definite preference for some kinds of work, which preference very often gives way later to quite other inclinations. A man ought, before he complains of having
missed his true calling, make sure that he could have
achieved more there than he does in his present place.

A second question is, whether the general belief is
true that having a work one likes insures greater efficiency. It is not so sure that this is always the case.
There have been quite a few instances of men being
really in love with their job and being not at all good
at it. Such a thing is well known of hobbies; many a
man is an impassioned fisherman or sailor or chess-
player without being the least of a champion. This
situation may be less frequent in regard to serious work,
but it occurs there too.

There is on the other hand quite a long list of instances proving that a man may be very efficient in some
work he does not like at all. A strict correlation between liking a job and being efficient in it does evidently

not exist. By this one is led to suspect that efficiency depends—given the necessary ability—on other factors than, or at least, besides inclination or disgust.

It is true, of course, that a man disgusted with his work will usually do it badly; but it is not equally sure that a man in love with his work will do it particularly well. It is indeed not enough to love one's work, one must love working too; and that is quite another thing. There are many people who love their work, who are even proud of it, but who nevertheless are not in love with working.

If men loved working—and there are quite a number who do—the problem of what kind of work they have to do loses something of its importance; many a man is to be found who is more or less indifferent to the kind of work he has to do, as long as it is work, useful and sensible, and as long as he is equipped to do it.

One understands easily why a man is dissatisfied with his work when he feels that it is not what he was trained for; but even in this case there are many who prefer any kind of work to idleness. But it is difficult to understand the mind of a man who has been very successful, who has work which is evidently suited to him and which he does very well, but which he does not like. Such cases exist. One may meet, for instance, a man who has gained a worldwide fame by his research work in science and who feels that he has missed his real job; he ought to have become a musician. He is indeed quite gifted for music, though not very much above the average; he probably would never have met with as much success as a composer as he has been awarded with for his researches in science. Everyone who knows him is aware of this fact, and he cannot be quite ignorant of it. Why, then, is he dissatisfied? There is only one explanation. This man is so exceedingly ambitious that even his having won the fame of being the greatest authority in his field can not quench his ambition. He finds a definite consolation in the idea that he would have still greater success had he been allowed to be a composer. Cases of this kind are not rare, though they may not be always as striking. But this fact supplies some subject for reflection. Could it not be that in many cases the dissatisfaction, arising from the idea of not having the right work to do, is in fact the effect more of the subjective state of thwarted ambition than of the objective fact of a disharmony of talent and work? A closer analysis of many cases of this kind shows indeed that ambition plays a very great rôle in the genesis of dissatisfaction caused by the kind of work.

There are many forms of work which in fact demand no special gift or talent. An average job can be done by a man with average talent, with average success. There is, of course, the exception of genius; some people are gifted in a quite special manner. Genius—or, at least, extraordinary talent—is not limited to art or science or statesmanship; there is a kind of genius also in less lofty levels of activity. Some people are, it seems, born with a quite peculiar gift for understanding mechanics, and there are others who understand, apparently without being in need of instruction, farming. They will achieve results very much above the average. But it is not for the majority to expect uncommon and exceptional achievements. Man has to know that he is a limited being. The idea of not having found the right job and of being better gifted for another one is indeed very often, as it was in the case of the famous scientist, but a way of getting some compensation for an unruly ambition.

We ought to be conscious that work is not for ourselves, in the first instance, but that it means essentially work for others. Every kind of work is therefore honorable and useful. And we ought to devote some thought to another fact too. The payment a workman receives depends largely on the amount and the quality of work he does. But his earnings are not the right standard by which to measure his work according to the principles of morals. There is the well-known parable in the Gospel, telling of three men who had been given each a certain sum of money; the first had received five, the second two talents, and the third but one. When their master came back, the first had gained five talents and thus delivered ten; the second, having gained two, delivered four. Both were praised by their lord and awarded in the very same manner and with the very same words. Which amounts to saying that not the absolute quantity of money earned was decisive, but the fact that both of them had doubled what they had been given. The third however had done nothing at all; he had hidden the money and gave it back, untouched. He was punished with extreme severity. Had he used the sum entrusted to him, he might have gained one talent and would have been rewarded as the other two were. He did not do so, because he felt that it was not worth while; he felt offended at not being given more, and therefore did nothing and met punishment instead of promotion.

Considered from the point of view of morals the important thing is not to do as much as another does, but to do as much as oneself is capable of doing. Or to express it in the language of the parable just quoted: it is important to earn the double, however large or small the original amount may be. It is wrong to introduce the standard of economics into things belonging to morals. The question of work is not merely one of economics; it has a definitely moral side too. There is no reason for being dissatisfied so long as one is sure of having done all one is capable of doing.

The enormous influence economics have gained over modern life, inevitable though it is, works towards abolishing our sense of moral standards. We become accustomed to judge of many things, especially of work and its success, only according to its monetary equivalents. There is a definite danger in this, and we ought to try to free ourselves from this one-sided view. It is probably impossible to uproot this wrong and disastrous way of thought in the great public; but every single man, having once become conscious of the utter falsity of this idea, ought to oppose it at least within his own mind.

4. *Obstacles to Perfection*

Many of the difficulties, perhaps most of them, which cause intense suffering and much trouble, arise, as has been shown, in social life and in relation to work. The attitudes causing those difficulties have but little to do with the immediate aspect of social connections or the conditions of work. Their sources spring from the depths of personality. Human personality is a unit; there are no "parts" in it existing, even relatively, in isolation; no side of personality is really detached from the rest; nothing in human personality can be influenced or changed in some way, without total personality becoming influenced and changed too, though this change sometimes may escape observations and is revealed only by a very close examination.

There are sides in personality or levels of it, which are more basic than others, notwithstanding the unity of personality. Work and social life, important though they are, do not constitute the most essential sides of personality. They are often the regions, so to say, where certain difficulties become most visible, but they are not the real essence of human life.

To make this point clear one must remember an old and fundamental statement of philosophy. Every being strives for the good. This striving for the good or the love of it is the great motive force driving the world along its path. This statement is true whether applied to human actions or to the processes going on within the world of inanimate things or to living beings devoid of reason and free will. This idea has been handed down to us from the wisdom of old pagan Greece, and it has been given a new and deeper meaning by the Christian Fathers and the Schoolmen of the Middle Ages. It can not be discussed here nor can the reasons for holding this view be made clear. There is, however, one side of this very large and complicated problem which has an immediate bearing on the topic this book is trying to explain. On this question which, though forming but a part of the general problem, is of an exceedingly great importance for human life, some words have to be said, because the practical side would be unintelligible without some previous explanation.

Among the goods all beings strive for, their own perfection holds a prominent place. Perfection means the actualization or the becoming really existent of all the qualities originally existing only potentially within the individual. The more perfect a thing becomes, the more visible its very nature becomes.

The term of striving has to be taken in a merely analogical sense in the case of beings which are not really capable of striving. But it is quite sensible to apply this term even to inanimate things, insofar as there is a definite tendency in nature to bring forth perfect things; this tendency indeed is often thwarted by circumstances; but whenever these are favorable we see this tendency at work. If temperature, concentration, purity and other factors are favorable, a chemical substance will appear in the shape of a beautiful crystal which indeed shows the nature of this particular chemical compound in a more perfect manner than does the amorphic state. The crystal is more perfect not only because it pleases the human eye by its symmetry and regular shape; it is a perfection in itself, because it realizes a property of the chemical body, namely, its capacity of appearing in just such a shape, which remains hidden as long as the body stays in its amorphic state. The striving for perfection becomes more manifest in living organisms; if a tree is not hampered by other trees, or deformed by storms raging around it, or by the inclemency of soil and climate, it will grow up very straight and develop symmetrically in every direction. A beautiful and well-developed tree is perfect in itself and not only because we love to look at it; rather, it pleases our eye, because it is perfect.

In living organisms some phenomena are observed which offer a rather striking similarity with striving as it is known to us by personal experience. Plants and certain lower animals are subjected to what biology describes as tropisms; this term signifies certain reactions conditioned by physical factors, as witness the turning of plants towards the light; the reaction mentioned is called, for instance, heliotropism. In higher animals there are complicated sets of reactions which tend towards the realization of certain aims and which are called instinctive reactions. Some of them serve the preservation of the individual; many of them, however, pursue aims far beyond individual existence and have to care for the preservation of the race. These reactions are not, of course, willed by the animal; the wasp depositing its eggs into the body of a caterpillar does not think of the food its off-spring will find there.

We may consider the tropisms and the instincts as a kind of rudimentary striving, so long as we do not fall into the error biology became guilty of during the nineteenth century, and do not believe striving and will and decision to be but transformed instincts. We do, in truth, not understand will and striving any better by calling them higher developed instincts; but we understand the nature of instinct by comparing it with our own conscious striving and considering the first as a rudimentary form—characteristic of the lower levels of life—of the latter. It is not easy to see how biology, and following it a certain kind of pseudo-philosophy, ever could overlook the fact that the lower and rudimentary forms of striving do not contain a single element which possibly would explain the development of the higher forms. The higher forms are richer in qualities than the lower; and enrichment necessarily implies some additional factors coming in, which can not be either explained by or derived from the lower and poorer forms.

It is well worth while to ponder just a little longer on this point. There is no more erroneous idea than that which may be aptly called the "view from below." According to this idea we have to "explain," for instance, mental life and moral demands by some mysterious development and complexity of biological phenomena. It is, however, easier to understand biological processes as some analogy of mental phenomena than to "explain" the latter by appealing to the former. All attempts to make psychology a chapter of physiology or to reduce mental life to brain functions have failed altogether. The brain is indeed the necessary instrument mind needs to manifest itself, but brain-cells and nerve-fibres are not the mind. All the boastful promises of which scientific and popular literature were full in the last century, are in truth empty phrases which one is amazed to hear repeated even today by men incapable of seeing reality and believed by others who have no power of judgment and not enough knowledge to see the truth.

All these grandiloquent words about the secrets of life being solved or going to be solved, have proved to be meaningless. We are today, after nearly a century of biological research, not one step nearer to the solution of the riddle of life, not to mention the secret of the mind.

The idea that the problems of humanity can be solved "from below" is as wrong as it is dangerous. The analyzing of the complex phenomena, finding out the "elements" building them up, and reconstructing the first after having thoroughly studied the second is possible only so long as we remain on the same level of reality; this is the procedure which is adequate in physics and in chemistry. But it does not apply the moment we step from one level to another, higher one. We can not "explain" life by means of chemistry or physics, nor can we reach an understanding of mental processes by means of biology.

The undue generalization of the methods of science has proved a disastrous mistake indeed. It has lead into the quite erroneous idea of reform—individual or social —having to start from below. Important though bodily health is for mental life, it is not sufficient to ensure moral health. Very strong, very healthy individuals, magnificent examples of the animal man, may be very imperfect beings from the point of view of morality; they may be even very immoral and become a much greater danger to society and humanity in general than weak and unhealthy individuals ever could be. It is the same with economics. Nobody will nor can deny that an improvement of the economic condition such a large part of humanity is laboring under is exceedingly necessary and indeed a moral demand; but it is wrong to believe that economic reform alone will prove efficient in creating a higher moral standard. We can not expect humanity to become morally better unless we realize the primary importance of moral reform. It is a mistake to believe that moral reform can wait until economic reform is completed. Humanity can not expect to make any efficient steps towards a better economic condition, unless moral improvement is considered at least as equally important.

Ensuring health and welfare to as great a number of individuals as possible is doubtless an aim worthy of the greatest endeavors. But neither individual nor social duties are limited just to the pursuit of welfare and health. The life of the single individual and the life of the community will improve only when the importance of moral progress is fully realized. Man is a unit of body and soul; it is not the sign of a scientific mind to deny this fact, but rather the effect of stubborn superstition and narrow-mindedness and blindness to the most obvious facts of reality.

There is a lot of talk today about physical education and quite enough discussion on mental hygiene. One is amazed at noticing the little interest paid to the problems of moral improvement.

Many people believe that morals as taught by the philosophy and the religions of old have become obsolete and useless. A new world, they say, needs new morals. Even a superficial examination of the new morals shows that they are not at all new; they are but parts of the old, leaving out some of the duties enjoined for nearly two thousand years. It had been said unto man: "Thou shalt love thy neighbor"; and there is no human being we are ever allowed to exclude, for there is no one who is not entitled to the name of neighbor. Modern morals say: "Thou shalt love thy comrades belonging to the same social class, or the people belonging to the same race." These "new" commandments are, as everyone ought to see, but restrictions of the old ones; there is nothing really new in them.

Moral imperfections, as measured according to the old standard of morality, are in fact very often at the bottom of many troubles. Though these troubles may become manifest in the first place within social life or in relation to work, their very origin often, indeed in the majority of these cases, has to be sought for in moral imperfections.

There can be no question of giving a complete list and an exhaustive description of all the various kinds of moral imperfections and their effect on individual happiness. The instances noted below will, however, be sufficient for supplying a general idea of the essential factors involved.

Striving must first of all know the goal it is going to pursue. Knowledge as such does not start action; this is done by will. But will has, before it can become active, or rather man, before he can begin to act, has to decide whether and how he is going to act. Even a quite insignificant action presupposes decision.

Difficulties in arriving at a decision are very frequent. They rank from a tendency to evade decision or to postpone it to a total incapacity of deciding at all. Indecision is closely related to doubt. People who are unable to make up their minds generally do not feel that they are incapable of doing so; they feel rather that they do not as yet see their way; if once they would know the surest and the best way, they would be quite ready to act; so at least they tell us. But in the meantime, they do not see clearly what has to be done, and they do, therefore, nothing at all. They call themselves prudent and despise other people because of what they call their imprudent haste. Haste is of course wrong too, though there are certain situations calling for quick action. True prudence and legitimate deliberation are, however, very different from lack of decision and unduly prolonged doubt.

By observing the behavior of a person addicted to long deliberation and protracted doubt a very curious phenomenon may be detected. Long as the preparatory period may be, no new thought turns up after the first five or ten minutes of reflection. In some rather rare cases indeed, an altogether new idea may suddenly turn up which opens a really new outlook. Generally it is the same sequence of thoughts which is run through over and over again. Nor does a person who has become the prey of this habit really hope for a new light which will help him make up his mind; he is quite aware of having got all the knowledge he ever will have. His idea of having to find out about the best way is usually but an euphemistic description of his not wanting, or not wanting as yet, to decide anything at all. If such a person is forced to decide upon a definite line of action, for instance, because he can not wait any longer, he very often has to confess—provided he is sufficiently sincere—that he could have decided long ago.

The real meaning of indecision or doubt is evidently not the wish for greater clearness, but the one to gain— or to lose, according to the point of view one takes— time. Doubt and the idea associated therewith, of not seeing clearly the rights and the wrongs of the case, are very efficient means for postponing and, eventually, avoiding action. These people will quite often let pass away the moment for decision, and they will feel definitely alleviated by having escaped decision, though they may, at the same time, regret not having taken a chance offered them. They were too conscientious, they could not act rashly, they had to consider every side— and then it had become too late.

There are, of course, situations which demand careful examination. Very few people have this presence of mind and this faculty of grasping at a moment's notice the essential factors which are necessary for forming a quick decision on behalf of important problems; this is a quality we admire in some famous characters of history, great leaders of men who knew when and how to take their chance. The average man, however, who is not gifted in this way, has to figure out what is best to be done. He has to do so because he is aware of the consequences his actions will have. He knows that he incurs responsibility; that by taking a wrong line of action he may imperil himself and others; he knows that great things are at stake, and that he has to act as best he can. But he knows too that he has to act anyhow, that he is not allowed to escape from action and that, accordingly, he has to take his risk.

Lack of decision means ultimately shunning responsibility. This is very probable from the first, since the result of the doubting attitude is evidently just this: either there is no action at all, and therefore no responsibility, or there is a plausible excuse at hand, in case the way chosen should prove to be wrong, because, says the doer, had he been given more time for deliberation, he would have found out what to do.

Man is very seldom allowed to abstain from action altogether. Some people indeed manage to do so. A minority—which is, however, quite large enough to cause serious apprehension—escapes action and responsibility by becoming ill, that is, by developing a neurosis which incapacitates them for work and all kinds of activity. The great majority can not avoid doing things and, accordingly, taking risks and incurring responsibility. They feel this to be very hard, and they find some alleviation—though they do not consider it to be one, rather the contrary—in their lack of decision. It helps them either to postpone action until they simply have to do something, and then they get the impression of having not had enough leisure for letting their decision mature. Or they let the right moment pass away and derive from this a consolation in case of failure. They always feel pressed, hurried on by circumstances, not allowed the necessary time, and thus have an excuse at hand when fate decides against them.

This attitude is essentially egotistic. These cunctatorian people do not fear, in truth, that something wrong could be done; they are only afraid that they could eventually have acted wrongly or have made a mistake. They do not consider the objective side of an action; they are interested in its results only so far as their own person is concerned. A student had once forgotten, or believed he had, to turn off the gas in the laboratory where he worked. He was afraid that he might start a fire. But he confessed that it did not matter at all to him whether the laboratory burned down or not, not even whether the inhabitants of the house were in danger; the only thing that mattered was whether he would be responsible. He was utterly indifferent to the objective side; neither the damage nor the danger interested him; so long as he had not committed a mistake, everything was all right. People do not, generally, speak out in so free a manner; but quite a few feel the same way. They wish to avoid any mistake whatever; they want, in fact, to be found absolutely faultless. But this is an aim not to be realized in this world; it is written that even the just man falls seven times a day.

This attitude is based on a great error. Things are, in truth, good or bad by their own nature and not only in regard to man and his judgment. The mistaken idea of goodness and truth depending on opinion has wrought more havoc in the world than one would imagine. Goodness or value, the goal every striving is aiming at, is primarily an objective quality of things or events. To man is given the task not of creating values or of attributing them to things originally indifferent as to value, but the task of discovering values existing in the world wherein he lives and of becoming aware of values as yet not real which he has to bring into existence.

Acting in a right way means nothing else but regulating one's actions according to the objective order of values, attempting to realize the highest good among those which can be realized in a given situation. By acting in this fashion the doer's personal value becomes greater; this is indeed but an accessory fact; it is not, nor ought it to be, the real motive of action. The value of an action is determined in the first instance not by the subjective moods preceding and accompanying it, but by the objective values it is meant to realize.

It is a great mistake to believe that certain mental states or moods are good in themselves, independent of the objects to which they correspond. This wrong idea finds expression in utterances like these: the ideas of Peter are of course quite wrong and even dangerous; but at least he is really enthusiastic about them; or: he devotes all his time to a pursuit which is indeed quite nonsensical; but he is so terribly earnest about it. These remarks imply that enthusiasm or earnestness are good in themselves, whatever the things may be one is enthusiastic or earnest about. Nobody will deny that it is quite right to be earnest or enthusiastic about things which by their own nature command such reactions. Enthusiasm or seriousness alone, however, without an object worthy of such sentiments is not to be admired, and a person wasting these fine feelings on unworthy objects is more to be pitied than to be praised or even only excused.

This ought to be very clear to everyone who devoted ever so little reflection to this matter. But there seems to exist a rather curious glorification of these sentiments independent of the objects to which they correspond. With many people it is not the object which justifies enthusiasm, but rather, on the contrary, it is the object which becomes heightened by being capable of arousing these feelings. Common though this idea is, it is nevertheless utterly mistaken.

Enthusiasm in the pursuit of a goal or as a reaction caused by some fact has become astonishingly rare in these our days. And if one ever comes across such a sentiment it is usually linked to things which objectively considered hardly deserve such a response. The wrong idea of the relation existing between the value of a thing and the subjective reaction is in fact very dangerous; it imperils, in an unsuspected degree, the soundness of the judgment on true values; it gives rise to an utter falsification of the idea man has of reality; it leads into error and trouble by overrating the importance of the subjective side of human behavior.

It is very easy to demonstrate how wrong this idea is; one has only to follow it to its last consequences. What about a criminal who is enthusiastic about his career as a murderer, embezzler, thief, or what not? Such things exist. People will indeed generally recoil from praising openly such a man's enthusiasm; but the often-used expression of "a great criminal," the glorification bestowed on certain types of lawbreakers in fiction and on the screen, and other features of the same kind easily observable in modern mentality denote a terrible decline in the true sense of moral values. This decline is not limited to moral values alone; the understanding of true value of whatever kind has definitely suffered today.

A man may think well of himself because he is conscious of devoting his energy to the pursuit of some goal he wants to reach, because he is indeed enthusiastic about it, because his whole personality has become wrapped up with his purpose. But there are but few people who care to find out whether these goals really deserve the spending of so much of energy, and whether it is right to let them occupy so large a place in life, or whether their objective importance justifies the mental reactions associated with them. This question is not asked because man loves to believe that objective values exist necessarily wherever his personal likings are engaged. This primitive attitude has been strengthened very much by the unlucky course philosophy has taken for more than a century. The philosophers have told mankind too often that there are no objective values, that values do not exist at all outside the human mind, that they are but the result of human predilection and the projection, as it were, into the world of reality, of the subjective attitudes. This idea finally became a general conviction. But its being accepted by a great majority—though one may notice today a movement away from this hopeless subjectivism—does not make this statement any truer.

Every being strives for the good. This may be used as a kind of definition of what is good or a value: good is what every being wants. This is quite true so long as it is taken in the right sense. Every striving indeed is significant of some good having been sighted. The study of strivings or of human wants may, therefore, well serve as a point of departure for an inquiry into the nature and the order of values. But it is absolutely wrong to conclude that striving creates, so to say, the value; in fact it is the value or the good existing in reality or capable of existing there which causes the wishes, the wants, the cravings and strivings of man to arise. Modern mind has become thoroughly imbued with the utterly mistaken idea of the subjectivity of values. This conviction has become so general that its presence is not even noticed any more. Quite a few people will profess openly their belief in the objective existence of values, because they see the strength of the argument; but they nevertheless let their behavior and their general attitude against life be influenced by the opposite idea.

Conscious or not, the attitude of subjectivism has got hold of the modern mind; and it supplies the soil in which grow many of the difficulties people experience. The unconscious subjectivism often double-crosses the purposes conscious reason forms and conscious will pursues. The result of this is a certain unsteadiness in the pursuit of recognized aims. The description by St. Augustine, quoted in a previous chapter, applies perfectly to this case; one will wants to realize aims which are recognized as objectively valid, while the second will obeys the secret subjectivism poisoning modern mentality.

The amount of egoistic ideas and feelings every man clandestinely indulges in is much larger than we like to acknowledge. The attainment of perfection, however, makes it necessary that these egoistic forces be overcome as far as possible. Discovering our hidden egoism is the first condition, if we want to make some progress on the road to perfection.

Many people claim that their making but little progress is not due to reasons within their own personality; they rather accuse circumstances. They know, for instance, that they ought to get on better with other people; but they find this to be impossible, because these other people will not desist from wounding their feelings, from behaving rudely, from being offensive, and so forth.

It is generally believed that sensitivity—the disposition of being easily offended, easily shocked and repulsed, of resenting intensely every slightest neglect or lack of consideration—that this exaggerated way of reacting on unpleasant experiences is a given and immutable feature of personality. The sensitive person knows perfectly that his life would be much easier if he would but get rid of this habit; but he is fully convinced of having been born with it and that he can not help being what he is. He is, in some measure, even proud of this quality; he believes it to be a proof of an unusually subtle and fine organization of his soul. He reacts more promptly and with a greater intensity than other people do; he is offended where another is not even annoyed; he is deeply wounded where another is not even touched.

Persons indeed differ in the subtlety of their souls. But it is very doubtful whether this kind of behavior denotes a real refinement of organization. The intensity of emotional reaction is not an absolutely reliable sign of such a finer structure of the soul. Nor is the strength of the visible reaction, not even the intensity of the emotions felt by the subject a trustworthy measure of the real depth of the emotions. One has, in truth, to distinguish two kinds of emotional set-up, which though similar in some respects are of a profoundly different nature.

There are, in English, two expressions, very much alike, but connoting nevertheless a different meaning; sensitivity and sensibility. Both come from the same etymological stock; they sound alike and are used promiscuously. It is, however, interesting to notice that the two adjectives related to these words have each a very definite meaning. Sensitive is given quite another signification than sensible; the connotation of reasonableness peculiar to sensible is rather instructive. Sensibility has something to do with reason or, at least, right ideas, while sensitivity seems to mean a merely emotional set-up.

Sensitivity is the name which we ought to reserve for the peculiar kind of behavior which has been sketched just before. Sensibility ought to signify exclusively a real refinement of perception of the values attached to persons, things, or events, and a personality set-up conditioning appropriate emotional reactions.

The sensitive person feels very strongly about all things touching his own personality; unfriendliness wounds him; lack of the consideration he feels entitled to offends him; being refused a favor he asks for depresses him; not being sufficiently regarded causes him intense suffering and makes him despair of humanity. But the very same individual may be utterly indifferent to the suffering of a third person. He may remain quite unmoved when hearing of the distress of others. The recital of some heroic deed leaves him cold. Anxious to see his own dignity acknowledged and his own demands granted, he may be quite ready to wound another's feelings and to disregard another's dignity. The intensity and subtlety of feeling of which he boasts and by which he suffers, enter into play only when his own personality and his own affairs are involved.

Sensibility, on the other hand, reacts with equal strength whether the individual's own person is involved or whether it is another's. A man gifted in this way feels deeply moved on hearing of another's calamities; his feelings are aroused by every fact worthy of emotional response. He is even more moved by things concerning other people than by those regarding himself. The sensitive person generally reacts intensely only on unpleasant impressions. Sensibility is a quality conditioning intense emotional response also to pleasant experiences. It enables a man to feel very vividly the beauty of things, the greatness of human acts, the values existing in the world surrounding him.

Sensibility has a close relation to the artistic temperament. Sensitivity, though often found in artists—because of their but too well developed vanity—has nothing to do, essentially, with this temperament. Sensibility is rather rare; it is perhaps a peculiar gift, though it can be developed up to a certain degree, by self-education. Sensitivity is a very common habit which, in fact, is good for nothing and which is a symptom of an exaggerated, if veiled, egoism.

A sensitive person wants others to behave according to a definite code of etiquette which, however, is not made public, but has to be guessed. Other people are expected to know, by a kind of intuition, how to behave; if they do not observe the rules laid down by the sensitive person and shut up within his mind, they are, so to say, deprived of his company and stricken from the list of his friends. Such a person behaves, in fact, like a reigning prince; whosoever becomes guilty of a breach of etiquette can not hope any more to be invited to the court. An average person can not, of course, eliminate people from his presence, like a prince is able to do; he can not banish them from his presence; but he can create a distance between himself and the offender, and that is exactly what the sensitive person does. He moves away from the offender, since he can not make him disappear.

A sensitive person suffers very much; there are so many opportunities to feel disregarded, offended, neglected. One should accordingly expect such a person to take great pains to avoid all encounters which possibly may cause suffering. By observing a sensitive person one gets, however, rather the impression that he is directly seeking for these painful experiences; he seems to be on the lookout for them instead of trying to escape them. He would fare better if he would try to interpret the actions and the words of his fellows in the friendliest possible way; by convincing himself that no offence was meant, he would indeed be spared many an unpleasant moment. Quite to the contrary, he is simply seeking for reasons which will justify his feeling offended; he has quite a trick of turning harmless words into an offence; he feels disregarded where no other person would think of such a thing. It is as if a sensitive person had a definite need of feeling unpleasant and of being wounded.

There are several reasons for this strange habit. In feeling offended we become aware of some personal rights having been violated. The sensitive person gets from the many opportunities of being offended an ever renewed certainty that he is entitled to a definite treatment, though his fellows deny it to him. But he could not feel wounded so deeply—this is more or less the way his thoughts would run, were they altogether conscious —if he were not entitled to a consideration greater than that which is granted to him. Though he complains of being neglected, of being not considered at all, of receiving a treatment as if he were just a mere nothing, he nevertheless derives from these experiences a curious kind of satisfaction.

A second reason for this oddity is that it gives still another opportunity for feeling superior. The sensitive person judges the behavior of the offenders to be utterly mean and improper; he himself would never behave in such a manner; at least he believes he never would, but he does oftener than not show an amazing thoughtlessness for the feelings of other people. This conviction, whether corresponding to reality or not, makes him feel definitely superior.

A third reason which makes the sensitive person suspect an offence where none was meant and where nobody else would think of one, is the basically distrusting and pessimistic attitude characteristic of this type.

Pessimism is a very serious handicap to perfection. It is very common and it is generally misunderstood. Pessimistic people believe that their way of looking at the world is due either to an inborn quality of their mind or to experience. Both ideas are wrong. Healthy children are never pessimistic; it is therefore not very probable that there is something like an inborn pessimism. This argument may not seem to carry much weight, since in a child there are many inborn but as yet undeveloped qualities which appear only later. Thus, there might be a congenital pessimism which becomes manifest only when the individual has grown up. Pessimism is indeed frequently observed during adolescence, where it results from the deep-seated changes personality is subjected to in these years. Normally, however, this pessimism is but a passing episode, brought about by the feeling of uncertainty, the doubts about the future, the insufficient knowledge of reality, the new experience of sexual life, and the like. In the average, young people will incline towards a more optimistic view. The pessimistic attitude during adolescense is closely related to definite experiences and states of development; pessimism in these cases can be easily understood as a reaction conditioned by these experiences. This fact makes it probable that in other cases too there is an understandable relation between experience and pessimism.

Pessimism is surely no primitive attitude. If it were, no progress would ever have been realized. Man must believe in the success of his endeavors to be successful; who doubts from the very outset, whether he will be able to achieve his purpose, is bound to fail. All the great achievements history tells of have been the work of optimistic people.

If we ask a pessimist why he holds so bleak a view, he has several answers ready. He tells us that by his pessimism he is spared disappointment; he is not shocked when things go wrong, since he never expected them to go right. He indeed says, when meeting failure: "I knew it beforehand," but he is nevertheless disappointed. Pessimism is in truth a merely superficial attitude; in the depths of human nature there is always hope and this hope never really dies. Even the pessimist is "hoping against hope."

The pessimist feels sure that he understands the world much better than does the optimist; he is disposed to look down upon the latter as possessing a shallow mind, a person ignorant of reality and incapable of seeing the truth. Thus pessimism gratifies the desire for superiority. If something goes wrong, the pessimist will triumphantly exclaim: "I told you so"; but he will forget to confess his mistake, if an enterprise has become successful.

According to the pessimist's ideas, experience fully justifies his point of view. He has been right so often; he has seen so often things taking a wrong turn; he found so many people who proved to be unreliable, did not keep promises, were untruthful, and so on; so many expectations were not realized, so many plans were frustrated, there was rain whenever he planned an excursion, the horse he bet on never won, places recommended to him were not pleasant, people he met were not nice, plays were not amusing, though he had been told they were and though he even had hope they would prove to be. Thus, he made during his life so many experiences which taught him not to expect anything but unpleasantness. Experience, however, depends on two factors; it is not merely the result of circumstances; it is formed, and very much so, by the person making it. A man may ride in a train which meets an accident; though he was not hurt at all, he becomes terrified and swears that he never again will go by the railway. Another man, having had the same experience, says to himself: "Well, that one and the same person becomes involved twice in a railway accident is rather improbable; now I may travel as much as I like without having to fear an accident." The same experience causes two very different reactions because the two personalities are different. There are, however, accidents which are not independent of one's personality. A railway accident is; an automobile accident may not be, because in this case presence of mind, attention, caution, and what not play a decisive rôle. Some people "have no luck"; this may be due to peculiar circumstances; but it may be —and often is—also the effect of certain peculiarities of the person himself.

The kinds of experience a man has depends to so large an extent on his personality that it does not prove anything about reality unless the peculiarities of personality have been taken into account. A despondent and pessimistic mind is incapable of discovering the good and pleasant sides of things, or if it does, it becomes aware at the same time of so many disadvantages that the assets become definitely outweighed. Such a person's thoughts always are of the "but" form: "This is quite nice, but. . . ." In fact, there is no chance of pessimism being ever really proved by experience. Nor are the pessimists in truth so thoroughly pessimistic as they believe themselves to be. They are quite optimistic at least in what regards the truth of their ideas. It is with them as it is with the sceptics; the sceptic doubts that man can discover truth, but he is sure that this statement made by him is absolutely true. The pessimistic philosopher holds that there is nothing really good in the whole world, except of course his own philosophy. Thus, the argument drawn from experience has no real weight.

All these reasons the pessimist alleges for justifying his point of view are but those of which he is conscious. By observing his behavior another reason may be detected, the strongest indeed of all. The pessimist knows beforehand that things are bound to go wrong. It were, therefore, but logical for him to refrain from all kinds of activity. But he persists in attempting enterprises,

notwithstanding his conviction that they are sure to
fail. He is forced into action partly by the necessities
of life; but he tries not infrequently things he needs
not do. He tries, though he is fully aware of his having no chances and of the odds being a thousand to one
against his being successful. The attitude of the pessimist can be best described by an allegory. Life appears
to him like a narrow path skirting a terrible abyss; a
bridge is in front of him, small and fragile, without a
rail, which crosses this abyss; beyond there is a dragon
hiding in a cave and all but too ready to thrust forth his
horrid head. (This allegory is taken, for that matter,
from a picture by the famous Swiss painter Arnold
Boecklin; its name is the Devil's Bridge.) The optimist
has of course to go the same way; but he is blind to the
abyss, he does not see the bridge; he has not the slightest idea of the dragon. A man now who goes this path
in full knowledge of its horrors and dangers is surely a
hero; but there is no heroism in passing through a world
of dangers so long as they are not perceived. The pessimist is a hero; the optimist is not—at least the pessimist feels this way.

A man secretly craving for an heroic life, for great
achievements, for adventures and victories, to whom
however fate denied such a rôle and whose courage
would not enable him to prove himself a hero in the
midst of real dangers, such a man can not do better than
to become a pessimist. Walking through a world of
dangers—though they are mostly created by his own
imagination, or at least very much enlarged by it—he is
able to feel a hero, without having to take the risks of a
really heroic life and without having to wait whether
fate will grant him an opportunity for heroism.

The great heroes, however, history describes and pos-
terity admires, seem to have been, more or less, rather

cheerful personalities. One will hardly find a grumbling, despondent, pessimistic personality among them.

Pessimism imperils perfection very much, because it makes a man blind to the real values and also to the real dangers. The attitude of: "Quite nice, but . . .," is not the right one whereby to discover the good and valuable sides of reality. The pessimist is aware, to an undue extent, of all the evils, but he is more or less insensible to the good and the beautiful. He can not, therefore, get any incitement for progressing towards and aiming at higher values, because either he does not see them, or if he somehow becomes aware of them, he does not believe in the possibility of realizing them. They are often to him but pleasant dreams imagined by humanity as a consolation and a compensation for an utterly unpleasant reality. The mist in which the pessimistic mind moves veils to him not only the far-off peaks he may admire without being able to reach them, but also the lower hills he may climb.

A person to whom the world presents such a dreary and colorless aspect needs must feel depressed and become incapable of all real joy. The only instance in which a true pessimist feels really glad is his having been right in his forebodings of evil. The "I told you so" of the pessimist denotes generally a definite feeling of triumph. Whenever he feels inclined to be glad because of something else, his pleasure is immediately spoiled by the afterthought that there must be some drawback. He is given a present and he thinks how badly he will feel should he lose it—and he is sure to lose it, since he has no luck. He admires a beautiful landscape in vacation time, and he thinks that he will have to leave in a fortnight; and that there will be bad weather the greater part of these two weeks.

The pessimist is quite unable to discover any good qualities in his neighbors. He does not see any reason why he should love them. Pessimism is surely one of the greatest obstacles in the development of love.

If pessimism is wrong, there is a kind of optimism which is in no way better. True optimism is not blind to the real dangers of life nor does it doubt that risks must be run. Life is, after all, an adventure and has to be lived as such. We never know for sure what the next day or even the next hour may bring. Adventures demand, however, not foolhardiness and haste; to meet them man needs a cool and clear head, a good knowledge of reality and of himself, a courageous mind and the power of endurance. Possessing these, he may trust that, with the help of God, he will achieve what he is asked to do. This is true optimism, and it is indeed very far from what people like to call by this name; when speaking of an optimist they generally think of a person who is thoughtless, rash, imprudent, rushing blindfolded into dangers. True optimism is not blind at all; it sees the dangers quite well, but it trusts that they will be overcome and it knows of the good chances too.

Optimism and pessimism are often believed to be due to temperament. One is, according to this view, born a pessimist or an optimist. It has been remarked already that a congenital pessimism probably does not exist. All men are born optimists; it is the natural attitude we ought to keep. And we are right in doing so, because we may trust in Divine Providence and Mercy, even though there is no absolute guarantee.

The idea of a congenital optimism or pessimism goes back to the teaching of Antiquity. The Greek distinguished four temperaments, and this theory became current also with the philosophers and physicians of the Middle Ages. The four temperaments played a great rôle in physiology and psychology even in later times; it is but a short time since this theory has become ques-

tioned and that other divisions of temperament have
been proposed. There is, however, anything but unanimity among the scholars on how the temperaments
ought to be classified. There is not even unanimity on
the question of the definition of temperament.

Temperament is best defined, as it seems, as a factor
influencing the formal side of behavior, but not the material side. Slowness and quickness, steadiness and unsteadiness of action, irascibility and coolheadedness,
energy and slackness, and many similar features depend
on temperament. Temperament may be the reason why
one person prefers melancholy music and another has a
liking for brisk and joyful pieces. But it is not, generally speaking, an effect of temperament whether a
man has a well-developed sense of duty, nor are his intellectual achievements dependent on temperament.

Temperament may, however, become indirectly influential also in regard to the material side of personality.
The choice of a job, for instance, may be influenced by
temperament. A man of little activity, slow in action,
disposed to rest and disliking exertion will feel repulsed
by jobs which attract a man of an opposite temperament. That is, he will do so, if he is inclined to humor
his temperament; but he may also, though this is surely
but rarely the case, feel that he ought to react against
his temperamental inclinations, be it because he hopes to
change his temperament by forcing himself in a way
opposed to it, be it that he is ready to take on himself a
lifelong struggle, because he believes it to be his duty to
follow a call, to undertake some work, or to help others.

This fact, rare though it is, proves that temperament
does not influence directly the material side of life or of
behavior; it does so only insofar as will allows it to gain
such an influence. The definition limiting the influence of temperament to the formal side of personality
seems therefore sufficiently sure.

Certain features of behavior which at first sight seem to depend on temperament may be, in truth, the effects of attitudes belonging to character. It has been explained already that, under certain circumstances, slowness in performance or impatience may be conditioned by the peculiar kind of pursuit of definite aims. In these cases behavior will change when the aims have become different. One gets then the impression of a change of temperament; but in truth there is no such change, since what has become different is the peculiar set of goals. Such observations do not prove that temperament in the true sense of the term may be subjected to change.

According to common opinion a person's temperament is a constant factor of his personality and one which remains unchanged whatever the outer conditions or the inner situation may be. But there is the fact, already alluded to, of repeated and sudden changes of temperament during adolescence. This seems at least to indicate, if not to prove, that one person may have during life more than one kind of temperament. We know also of cases in which a thorough change of temperament occurred as a consequence of certain experiences. The loss of an exceedingly loved person may change a cheerful temperament into a melancholy one; a man given to despondency, distrust and pessimism can occasionally become altogether different when love finds the way into his heart. There is, in truth, no real proof of temperament being essentially immutable. This idea springs partly from undue generalizations, partly from certain suppositions which are far from being evident.

The question of temperament and the chances of it being changed have to be discussed here at some length because temperament is very often alleged as an excuse for not making progress on the way of perfection.

It is true that real changes of temperament are observed but rarely. But the very moment even only one case of change of temperament has been ascertained, the theory of the essential immutability of temperament becomes untenable. There is no saying more nonsensical than the one that no rule is without exceptions. Exceptions do not prove a rule, they disprove it. General statements of a negative character are, let it be said once more, disproved even by one single positive instance. There are cases of real change of temperament; the idea of immutability has therefore to be abandoned.

It may be that in many cases the conditions necessary for a thorough change of temperament can not be found. But even if temperament can not be changed, it can at least be brought under control.

The influence of temperament on behavior and its importance as an obstacle varies according to the kind of temperament. It would be indeed a great help if we possessed a reliable and complete division of temperament. The old classic division seems still to be the best, the more as modern psychology has not been able as yet to replace it by a better one. The old classification distinguishes four types of temperament: the sanguine, the choleric, the phlegmatic, and the melancholic temperament. The names come from the idea the physicians of old held, that temperament is due to the composition of the fluids of the body. Choleric means, for instance, that there is an abundance of bile; melancholic, that the bile is unusually dark.

The main feature of the sanguine temperament is a certain elasticity of the mind. It swings, as it were, between elation and depression; but its average color is one of cheerfulness. Difficulties may cause a momentary dejection, giving way however soon to a hopeful attitude. The danger peculiar to this temperament is a certain superficiality and shallowness, giving birth to the wrong optimism mentioned above. The sanguine person is apt to neglect the unpleasant, even the serious sides of reality and, by this, to develop a mistaken idea of life. These people are not easily discouraged; their optimism and the tendency of making light of difficulties may lead them, on the other hand, into foolhardy enterprises. They are genial companions, sociable, inclined to see the humorous side of things, without being malicious. Because they are easily contented they often lack the will for strenuous exertion and are inclined to give up, not because of discouragement, but because they do not take things seriously enough or because they so think them worth while.

The choleric temperament is characterized by fits of energy and passion. Persons of this type are rather emotional, quick to anger and enthusiasm, but quick too in letting their energy abate. They are capable of great exertions, provided that these do not last too long; the quiet energy of endurance and persistence is but poorly developed. These people are easily moved to rash action; they are apt to flare up in anger because the first impression is so strong with them that they have not the time to consider whether it is correct or not. They are, accordingly, in danger of becoming unjust and offending; they are disposed to leave things unfinished because their energy, great as it was when they started, did not carry them over a longer period of exertion.

The phlegmatic temperament is just the opposite of the choleric type. Its outstanding feature is an undisturbed and undisturbable equanimity. The phlegmatic is not easily aroused to action; many things which cause the choleric and even the sanguine to become active, leave the phlegmatic cold; it needs quite a lot to stir him up. By this emotional torpidity he escapes a good many unpleasant experiences, but he misses many pleasures too. He is, however, sometimes capable of a rather marked tenacity, of pursuing a goal in a quiet and stubborn manner. The danger peculiar to this type is, of course, indifferentism, an unwillingness to acknowledge the importance of things, a tendency to level down values. Such a person may be quite ready to recognize theoretically the existence of higher values, though he does not feel like striving for them. He often gives the impression of laziness, though he is not really lazy; inactivity and laziness not being necessarily identical. His capacity of perceiving the objective order of values may afford a basis for overcoming his phlegma which indeed gives way sometimes, when really great interests are at stake, to a not seldom astonishing activity.

The melancholic temperament is, at least when it is somewhat developed, doubtless the most serious handicap of every kind of progress, be it in the line of work or of social achievements or of moral perfection. The melancholic habit of the mind creates easily a very far-going falsification of reality, obliterating therein, as it were, all the positive values. The melancholic is not, unless his temperament is verging already on pathological states, incapable of perceiving the higher values; but he is obsessed by a deeply rooted doubt whether they can become real at all. There is indeed goodness— but it is a mere idea; you may cross the whole world and never meet it. There is the ideal of altruism and disinterestedness; but who ever saw a really disinterested and altruistic person? The melancholic is essentially pessimistic in his outlook on life; his temperament is indeed the soil on which the seed of pessimism grows best. The melancholic's pessimism embraces the world as well as his own personality; no good can ever come from either of them. The world is bad and he has no luck; ill-fated stars rule over his life. He is not aware that at least one-half of his ill-luck is of his own making. He never finds fault with himself; other people or circumstances are the only reasons for his misfortunes. He is never guilty, though his "unhappy temperament" may have something to do with his not getting anywhere; but his temperament is beyond his power; he can not help being what he is. If he but knew what he really is, he would try to change. The melancholic is in fact a full-grown egoist. He, like every one, wants to be happy and successful, but he is not willing to pay the price. He wants happiness to be a gift granted to him, not as the fruit and the premium of exertion. The melancholic is exceedingly exacting; no proof of love, of regard, of reverence even is great enough; he is insatiable. No wonder he has lost his courage, since what he is after is in truth beyond his and every man's reach; no wonder he is pessimistic, because he had to be disappointed, having asked for more than man ever will receive; no wonder he has no initiative and no persistence, since he knows in the depths of his personality that he will never be given what he wants, because his wishes transcend the limits set to human nature. The melancholic temperament is in truth the greatest handicap and the greatest danger on the road to perfection.

It is the more dangerous because it so often assumes the aspect of prudence, of wisdom, of religiosity. Is it not said that we are dwelling in a "valley of tears"? That we are staying there "weeping and sighing"? Who, then, will blame the melancholic for being what he is? These are in truth but petty excuses. It is written also: "Rejoice, and again I say, rejoice." Nowhere have we been taught to creep along with bent necks and doing nearly nothing at all. Not one passage in the Gospels is to be found where we are told to brood and to grumble and to deplore our unhappy fate; but it is said that we ought to do something; "Go and teach all the people; whatever you have done unto the least; take your cross and follow; great is the harvest and small the number of workmen," and so on. Melancholic idlers are just a nuisance, a burden to their relations and friends, good-for-nothings in society, inefficient at work, egoists who spend their whole time and all their energy on staring at their own picture, concerned exclusively with their own personalities.

The differences between the temperaments become clearly visible in situations where decision is difficult and action unavoidable. The attitudes of the representatives of the four temperaments may be described thus: The sanguine says: "Sure, it's difficult, but it will come out all right"; the choleric: "I must and will be successful"; the phlegmatic: "There is after all a chance, let's try"; the melancholic: "I have to do it, though no good can come from it."

"Pure" cases of these four types of temperament are very rare; there is usually some element belonging to another type mixed with the prevalent temperament. The descriptions given above are, accordingly, somewhat overdone, though the picture drawn of the melancholic is nearly true to life. The attitude against success and defeat reveals which temperament prevails within a personality.

The sanguine is seldom or never pessimistic; he may talk in this vein for a short time, because he is just depressed by some misfortune, but this mood will not last. He does not lose his courage, unless he be broken—as everyone may be—by a load too heavy to carry. The phlegmatic is neither really an optimist nor is he a pessimist; he is rather indifferent. Success does not mean much to him, nor failure either. He is capable of sticking, if he thinks it worth while, stubbornly to his plans and to his duty. People of this type are often very courageous, though they do not care, as a rule, to make use of this quality. The choleric may lose courage quickly; but the next fact appealing to his impassioned

soul will rouse him to action again. If the temperament of the sanguine may be likened to a steel spring
which may be curbed, but regains its shape the very
moment the pressure is lifted, the temperament of the
phlegmatic is more like a storage battery which after
having been discharged regains after a time its former
voltage. The melancholic has no courage to lose, because he has none at all. What sometimes may impress
an observer as an act of courage is at the best one of
despair. He is croaking evil, prophesying misfortune
for himself and for others. He is unwilling to move,
because he knows that all will be in vain. Such a man
ought to be very glad if some little success comes his
way, since he did not believe in success at all. But no;
he is not satisfied; the little success does not mean anything to him; he deems it a failure, because no average
success is good enough for him. Successes that would
content the melancholic do not exist in average life.
He wishes a first-class, an unheard of success, one the
like of which never has been before. The melancholic is
indeed as ambitious as he is cowardly. Both his qualities, his greediness for success and his lack of initiative
become very serious obstacles to perfection.

Success is not identical with achievement, nor is failure the same as defeat. The confusion of these terms is
very common and has rather evil consequences. Success and defeat are terms belonging to the language of
ambition. Achievement and failure are facts belonging
to the realm of reality. There are successes which are
no achievements; a student may pass an examination by
cheating; the success is undoubtedly his, but not the
achievement—at least not in regard to scholarship,
though it might be quite an achievement in another
line. There are, on the other hand, many achievements,
and there have always been such, not crowned by success. The history of science and of art knows quite a

number of these instances. A man may fail to achieve his purpose because of circumstances independent of his personality; this is failure, but it is not defeat of which he had to be ashamed. Such a failure becomes a defeat only in the eyes of one who is foolish enough to believe that he ought to overcome any obstacle whatsoever and neglects the fact that he is but a human being and not an incarnation of omnipotence. One has to know that reality will prove stronger than man over and over again. Progress is achieved only by "trial and error," and error means failure. It is of an overstrung and exaggerated ambition to consider failure as an equivalent of defeat.

Such an overstrung ambition needs must lead to disappointment. The habit of being easily disappointed is another serious handicap to perfection, because of its detrimental influence on courage and because of the conclusions the human mind usually draws from such experiences. Everybody agrees that it is quite "natural" to feel disappointed whenever something goes wrong. But man has not to be "natural" in this sense of the word. Even if abstraction is made from what, theologically, is called supernatural life, there are higher forces and higher interests alive in the mind which are, in a certain degree, opposed to the "natural" tendencies. It is, for example, not "natural" to man to work or, at least, to work more than mere maintenance of life necessitates; but there is some mysterious force which urges man onwards, and he has, in obeying this urge, to resist his "natural" inclination towards laziness. Egotism is very "natural" too; but the necessities of social life and a sense of duty, whose presence can not be denied, make man act against his "natural" desires. In the same way it is "natural" to feel disappointed, and there is nevertheless something wrong in this habit. To uproot it is probably impossible; the important thing is to know what is beneath it and to attempt to subdue this inclination.

Why are men disappointed? The fact that things are not developing as we expected them to do is not sufficient to explain the peculiar note of disappointment. There is something more in our hope that things will turn out according to our wishes; there is a dumb but definite idea that they have to, that we are entitled to see our expectations come true, that the world has simply to follow our ideas as if they were the very laws governing reality. Reason, of course, disapproves of such ideas which therefore do not dare to come forth into the light of clear consciousness; but they are nevertheless very active and very influential.

Man may wish for everything which is reasonable and for a good many things that are not. There is no great danger in wishing. It becomes, however, dangerous the very moment wishes become transformed into demands. There is a great difference between wishing and demanding, though this difference is often not noticed at all. Wishes may be granted or not; we are pleased by the first and displeased by the second, but neither the one nor the other has a great influence on our behavior. But we make fulfillment of demands a condition of our behaving as we ought. We act, though we do not always speak, in a way as if we said: "First I have to get this and then I will do that." But we have no right to bargain with fate; we have to do our duty regardless of the fact whether our wishes are fulfilled or not. For once Frederick Nietzsche was right when he wrote: "It is for us to keep the promises life makes to us."

Behavior is very much influenced by the voluntary and the emotional sides of personality. Great as their importance is, there is still room for reason to become influential too. Reason does not exercise an absolute dictatorship over will; man can always act in opposition to what reason tells him. But he can never decide for any line of action unless reasons presents to him the aims to pursue. When reason fails, when its judgment becomes unreliable, action will necessarily go wrong. Ignorance and error are dangerous stumbling-blocks on the way to perfection.

It is, accordingly, man's duty to develop reason and to acquire knowledge. It is dangerous to trust to "feeling" as is commonly said. Feelings, or rather intuitional knowledge, are difficult to test; they may be right, but they may be also quite wrong.

Modern times have developed a certain lack of esteem for reason and intellect. Many people believe, and quite a few so-called philosophers teach, that intellect destroys the spontaneity of human nature and gives the mind a quite wrong idea of reality. Thought is considered as something secondary; instinct has come to be looked at as the true guiding light of human life. Intellectualism is decried as one of the greatest errors mankind ever made; anti-intellectualism and what they call irrationalism are hailed as the panaceas which are going to save mankind and to restore its original contact with reality.

There may be something wrong with an exaggerated rationalism and intellectualism, though they are probably still less dangerous than indulging in a blind faith in instincts. A true reverence for reason and a correct use of intellect are still more reliable guides through the mysteries of reality than their contraries. The condemnation passed, not without reasons, on intellectualism and rationalism has been unduly generalized so as to include the legitimate and inevitable use of the intellectual faculties.

This modern tendency of a wholly unwarranted disparaging of intellect supplies a good excuse for all those people who are recoiling from the task of intellectual perfection. It ought to be clear, however, that man has the duty to cultivate whatever faculty he is given. There is no reason for remaining uncultured and uninstructed if the opportunity for enlarging one's mind is at hand.

But here again ambition becomes an obstacle. Not the only one, indeed, since quite a few feel a strong reluctance against intellectual endeavor, though they may be willing to undergo great physical exertions. One really wonders why. One reason is surely that the results of physical work and training are so much more visible. The progress a man makes when going in for some sport or learning how to handle a machine can be controlled nearly every day. It is different with intellectual work. There is but little satisfaction to be gained from taking account of the number of pages read or written, because one is never quite sure whether one understood the text or whether one's work is of some worth. It is for this reason that people like to pass an examination, even if they need not, nor ever will use the certificate; but they value it as a tangible proof of their having really acquired knowledge.

Many people behave, in face of intellectual endeavor, very much like the man spoken of in an earlier chapter who built his house in the midst of a great plain. Or they behave—in this case as in many others too—like the famous fox of the fable who found the grapes too sour because he could not reach them.

This fox has, however, two cousins worse than he. The one, finding himself in the same fix, says: "Funny, how could I be so deceived? These are no grapes at all." For the sake of not having to recognize the limits of his power he falsifies reality. So did, for that matter, the first fox too, though in a lesser degree, since he called the grapes by their name.

The third of this clan, faced by the impossibility of getting at the grapes, said: "What an idea of mine to

try to reach these fruits; I never really liked grapes."
This one goes so far as to lie to himself.

The family-name of these foxes may be Smith or
Jones or any other name. They are indeed to be found
everywhere. The second and the third are worse than
the first, because they deviate even more from truth
merely to save their pride and vanity.

The attitude of the foxes leads to an upsetting of the
true order of values. Things are either credited with
some unpleasant quality they perhaps do not possess;
or their true nature is denied; or they become disquali-
fied and deprived of their objective value.

This way of transforming reality so that it will suit
an individual's personal likings and views becomes particularly manifest in regard to intellectual and cultural
values. People who do not feel equal to getting hold
of these things or to whom the opportunity is denied
by circumstances, are very often inclined to despise
what they cannot reach. Sometimes a definite feeling
of envy is mingled with this attitude, especially when
people see that others become famous or are earning
money or are able to do great things by what they know
and can. But to an incredibly large majority, preferring
a string quartette by Mozart to the latest "hit" song,
the poem of Dante to the newest "thriller," two hours
of quiet reading to a baseball game is just a craze or a
sign of snobbishness. A song, a detective story, a game,
all these things have of course a definite value of their
own and occupy a place in the order of values. To
deny this would be indeed snobbish. It is, in fact, not
less wrong to overlook values belonging to a lower level
than to deny those of the higher levels. Recognizing
the objective order of values means that every value is
recognized and placed where it belongs.

The disrespect in which so many people hold the
higher values is born, last but not least, from a feeling

of incapacity—just like what the foxes feel. Instead of simply and honestly accepting the fact, man denies the existence and the importance of values he believes beyond his reach. By this he bars more than ever the way leading to them. His idea of being incapable of understanding and enjoying them is often a mere prejudice. Many a man would derive quite a noticeable amount of pleasure out of these things did he but dare to approach them. The reluctance to do so as well as the judgment passed on them is oftener than not the result of training and education and not due to a real deficiency of the individual's personality.

The average man is probably gifted with a capacity for enjoying intellectual, artistic and cultural values greater than he believes. But he is kept back from finding out how far this gift will carry him by the fear of not equalling the "high-browed" people; a second hindrance is made up by certain current ideas and the slogans expressing them which indeed poison the intellectual atmosphere.

Believing in such slogans and accepting, uncritically, ideas spread by propaganda, which is very often far from being disinterested, is another serious obstacle. In assenting to ideas and theories on politics or culture, on religion and art, or on life in general we ought to be very careful. Many ideas appeal to us not because of their evident truth, but because they humor our prejudices or suit our desires. A theory defending the idea that prisons are immoral institutions and that punishment is detrimental to the nation's welfare would be very much applauded by the inmates of prisons. Such an applause would not be, however, the expression of a rational conviction or the result of an ascertaining of truth. Abolishment of private property sounds agreeable to the ears of the destitute classes, and disagreeable to those of the capitalist. But neither pleasure nor displeasure are reliable signs of truth or falsehood. Truth is independent of assent and dissent. A statement is true or false by its own nature, and its being accepted or rejected does not add anything to its truth or untruth. The approval an idea meets with a great majority may be a reason for inquiring into its merits, but it is never a proof of its truth. Both history and observation show that the greatest falsehoods have been occasionally and still are universally applauded.

It would be better if mankind were less liable to suggestion by slogans and by propaganda. Individual life and individual progress would profit indeed quite a lot by a greater use of conscientious criticism of ideas.

There is a peculiar danger in so-called new and modern truths. Many people become enthusiastic about ideas simply because they are new and because the actual situation—in politics, economics, science, etc.—is felt to be unsatisfactory. Many people believe themselves obliged to side with the latest "truths," because they are new and "modern." There is a definite and dangerous allurement in modernity. One wants to be up-to-date and does not like to be considered a reactionary. But reaction depends in its value upon the thing it reacts against; and sometimes it is very necessary to be a reactionary. Modern, on the other hand, means *modo hodierno,* according to the fashion of today; what has been modern yesterday may be obsolete tomorrow. There are many striking examples of this in every region of human life. A scientist who refused, in the eighties of the last century, to believe in Darwinism was decried as a reactionary and as incapable of understanding the newest and most modern "truth." Today a great majority of biologists have ceased to believe in Darwinism or even in the theory of evolution.

Life becomes easier, it is true, by a ready acceptance of current ideas. In taking over what is just the belief of a majority or a group, man is spared the task of finding out by himself about truth and untruth. His responsibility too becomes less; he relies on what his neighbors believe or on what his paper tells him. Nor does he thus run the risk of having to defend his own ideas or to oppose those of his friends and comrades. All this is not without its advantages. But it is not the right thing to do.

A blind rejection of new ideas is, of course, not better than blind acceptance. We ought to consider earnestly whatever new "truth" is presented to us. Clinging to prejudices is a very bad thing. A famous physicist is said to have remarked: "I believe only in what I see; and I do not care to look at things which I do not believe." What this man stated rather bluntly expresses indeed the attitude of many people on behalf of new ideas. No doubt that this attitude is quite wrong.

There is in quite a few of us a very marked tendency for opposition. We oppose not because we have made sure of the falsehood, but just because we feel like opposing. This habit springs, at least partly, from an exaggerated will for self-assertion. The opponent is always noticed; he may be unpleasant, but he can not be overlooked. He is often credited with originality, though he deserves this qualification but seldom. Opposition gives rise to debates and to discussions which, especially when becoming rather fierce, interrupt the monotony of every-day life. Opposition is one of the means by which to procure more or less sensational experiences.

There are many minds possessed by a craving for unusual and sensational experiences. The pleasure found in "thrillers" or in witnessing a boxing-match or in hearing of some catastrophe or a crime springs from this source. These things have been discussed already in an earlier chapter. The same desire for unusual emotions and a change of monotony is at the bottom of another wide-spread habit which is apt to imperil progress; since it gives rise to a thoroughly distorted idea of reality; that is sentimentality.

Sentimentality is not easily defined. It can perhaps be described as the habit of apparently strong emotional reactions on occasions which objectively do not warrant them. The emotional display is often very impressive. But it is not sure at all that the emotions are as strong as they seem to be; they are, in fact, notwithstanding the impressiveness of the utterances, rather shallow.

The behavior of a sentimental person is, in many ways, rather like the one described before in sensitive people. There is one feature common to both habits: the range of emotional reactions is restricted in a very curious manner. The sentimental person will shed tears where no average man would think of being moved in this way; but the same person may remain quite unmoved and cold in face of things which ought to appeal to every normal person. Sentimentality does not care, in fact, for the true values and the real importance of the things; it is interested not in things, not in objective reality, but exclusively in subjective states of mind. Not the object which moves but the being moved is the one important thing to such people. Therefore, they are definitely greedy for emotions and try to procure them wherever they can.

Sentimentality ignores the existence of objective differences between facts or events exercising an emotional appeal. Every unpleasant fact becomes a catastrophe, every slight misfortune becomes a tragedy, every little rippling on the surface of the emotional life becomes an impassioned reaction, tears flow at the most insignificant occasion, each nice thing is a marvel, hardly interesting news becomes exciting, and so on.

The habit of exaggerated emotional reactions blunts the discernment for values. It creates a tendency towards considering all events as equally important; since the emotional reaction is nearly always at its utmost height, there is no possible gradation. The death of a pet, say of a goldfish, releases such a flood of tears that the death of a mother can not produce a greater one. Sentimentality tends to create a wrong idea of values. There are people who feel the greatest pity for dogs and cats and horses and birds; the same people are quite cold to the fact that there are children starving, sick persons not cared for, large masses without the primitive benefits of culture. Sentimentality usually is quite content with its emotional responses; it does not care for letting them become motives of action. All the energy is spent on emotion, no part of it is left for action.

The uniformity of emotional reaction, regardless of the objective differences of reality, is absolutely wrong. This habit is a real evil; it ought to be exstirpated as thoroughly as possible. Reality is not uniform; there are different levels of existence and, accordingly, of value. To confuse them, as the sentimental person is apt to do, amounts to a distortion of truth. Sentimentality is an enemy of truth. Progress and perfection, however, are based on the acknowledgment of truth.

There is one truth man is very unwilling to accept or even to discover, the truth about himself. To see himself as he really is, he needs indeed some very strong incentives. This question is, however, so closely linked with the problem pertaining to the sphere of religious life that it is better discussed under this heading.

5. Handicaps of Religious Life

Some few introductory words seem necessary. It has been explained already in the Preface that this book can not be called a religious one in the strict sense of the term. It is written from the point of view of the psychologist and it avoids carefully all strictly theological arguments. But the psychologist is not allowed to neglect the religious side of human life, this side being of enormous importance. Some modern psychologies which believe that they may discard altogether the notion of a spiritual soul are because of this prejudice exceedingly unsatisfactory. They do not afford a real help in the difficulties of practical life, nor do they give any consistent idea of human nature. That man is a unit of body and soul is not a mere idea, not a belief dictated by faith, but a fact which can be proven by a careful analysis of mental life. The very moment, however, the existence of the soul has been ascertained, it becomes clear that this soul must be of a spiritual nature, and by this we become sure, too, that the soul belongs, so to say, to another world besides this tangible one we are living in. Introducing the notions of a soul and its supernatural destination is not at all "unscientific"— though quite a few psychologists and philosophers would have it be so—but simply the result of unprejudiced observation and conscientious analysis of facts. The psychologist is forbidden to encroach on the domain of theology; but he cannot disregard the facts of religious life. He has, therefore, not only the right, but even the duty to say whatever his science may tell him on the psychology of religious life and its difficulties.

Notwithstanding, however, the importance of the subject it deals with this chapter will be rather short. Partly because many problems must be left to theology to discuss them, partly because a great deal of what has been said in the foregoing chapters applies equally to religious life. There is probably no imperfection, no fault, no undesirable habit which does not influence religious life somehow. Though many of them become visible mostly in other sides of personal life, they are not without influence on religious life. This ought to be clear, because human nature is essentially a unit, which knows not of real "parts." It is, accordingly, a mistake to believe that certain faults are without any importance for religious progress. There are surely some whose influence on religious progress is rather small; but hardly any which have no influence at all.

Nearly all the faults or bad habits which have been discussed in the earlier chapters go back either to an exaggerated love of oneself or to an unwillingness to acknowledge truth. But religious life is based mainly—when looked at from the psychologist's point of view—on screwing back self-love to the right level and on recognizing truth. This being the case, it is evident that the faults discussed until now can not be indifferent to religious progress. There are, however, some things which influence religious life in a more direct manner.

Faith is belief in revealed truth. Superstition is, therefore, the absolute opposite of true faith. Curiously enough, some people manage to believe in the teachings of religion and to be superstitious at the same time. They are either not aware of the striking contradiction of faith and superstition, or they do not understand what superstition really is.

Religion, of whatever kind, teaches man to acknowledge his smallness, his insignificance, his helplessness and to turn to God's grace and mercy for help, to trust in Divine Providence for disposing all things as is best. Humility is, therefore, the very basis of the religious attitude.

Superstition acts quite differently. Its true nature is

pride and an undue exaltation of the position held by man within the universe. Superstitious belief and behavior can be divided into two classes. Superstitious people either believe that they can, by some "magical" procedure, influence destiny and fashion it according to their own wishes, or they feel convinced that they are, in some mysterious way, warned of dangers or advised how to act. The first group indulges in magical practices, the second trusts in forebodings. Carrying amulets, touching wood for the sake of avoiding misfortune, making "the horns" to paralyze "evil eye," all these procedures belong to magic. Avoiding traveling on Fridays, being thirteen at table, etc., is but the reverse of magical practice. Taking a black cat that inadvertently crosses one's way as a presage of evil may serve as an instance for the second kind of superstitious belief.

The use of magical tricks is based on the quite presumptuous idea that man may acquire some knowledge enabling him to influence the course of things. Magic lets man take the place of the Almighty Himself. The magician is credited with supernatural power far beyond what is conceded to man. To him the real master of the world is not blind fate, as the heathens of old thought, nor Divine Wisdom, as Christianity teaches, but man insofar as he possesses some secret knowledge and power. It is not necessary to point out at greater length that this attitude denotes indeed a pride as unruly as unfounded. Pride which, according to the saying of Dante, was the first beginning of all downfall, has always been and still is the soil on which grows the ugly and poisonous plant of superstition.

Belief in forebodings and signs is of the same nature. Man feels sure that Fate or Providence will trouble to send him a special message whereby to regulate his actions. By this he becomes certain that he holds quite a peculiar and eminent place; else the superhuman powers would not care to warn him. The black cat does not portend evil to everyone whose path it crosses; only to him who knows how to interpret this sign; he is picked out, as it were, and the pet of these unknown powers.

This indeed still quite superficial analysis of superstition proves sufficiently that between true faith and superstitious belief there is an unbridgeable abyss. Faith can never be identified with superstition; the so very "enlightened" people who are accustomed to do so are either incapable of understanding the nature of faith or blinded by prejudice. Superstition can never become reconciled to faith. There is an absolute incompatibility.

Superstitution may appear in many cases as a rather innocent foible. It may be one, since it is not so much superstition itself as the basic attitude supporting it which is so absolutely incompatible with faith. Anyone who wants to be true to faith and who detects within his mind an inclination towards superstition or some habits pertaining to it had better be warned and submit his conscience to a careful examination; he is sure to discover an unthought-of amount of hidden, unruly and even unhuman ambition.

Superstition is a trickish method for escaping a situation which is as inevitable as it is painful; that is the simple and wholehearted acknowledgment that law governs human life and is stronger than human will. Life is full of the everlasting battle of human will against these laws. Self-assertion is a normal feature of personality; man can not do without it, because did he so he would simply be crushed. This attitude—provided it stays within the proper limits—is not only necessary to keep man alive, but it is morally right too. Our own personality represents a value of its own of which we have, paradoxical though it may seem, to take care. Personality is not something given to us as a ready-made thing; it is rather something entrusted to us as a task. Man finds himself as a kind of raw material out of which he has to fashion a respectable personality.

Man has to find a middle way between indulging in an unruly love of himself and abandoning his task of forming his own personality. This middle way can not be discovered by means of a compromise. A compromise is always a poor solution; what is needed is something more than a mere compromise; it is a real synthesis which is not only between, but also above the two extremes.

There have been always and there are today too, certain people who decry the middle way as mediocre and as unworthy of man. They hail extreme measures; they are radicals. To them the radical alone deserves to be called a man in the full sense of the name.

This idea which in modern times has found but too many admirers is far from being clear. It is rather misty because it is often based on a perilous confusion of two terms of which the outward manifestations may be rather alike, though their nature is not at all the same. There is radicalism and there is intransigency. Radicalism implies an utter one-sidedness, linked to an absolute incapacity of seeing another's point of view or at least to a determination to ignore it. Reality, however, is not one-sided; the radical or extremist view is accordingly necessarily wrong. Intransigency means the unwillingness to make concessions once the truth has been ascertained. A radical is of course intransigent; but an intransigent person is not necessarily a radical. One may be very intransigent in defending a moderate view. The attitude of the Church throughout the centuries since her foundation is a striking example thereof. The Church never made, nor will she make any concessions; in regard to the truth she preaches she is utterly and thoroughly intransigent; but she has never been addicted to radicalism. She does not teach, for instance, that all men are equal, nor that there are essential and unbridgeable differences; she does not believe man to be "born good" as J. J. Rousseau taught, nor does she hold him to be "radically bad" as some Protestant philosophers and theologians will have him to be.

To follow the middle way is not at all to make shallow and cowardly compromises. The faith the Church enunciates is anything but a compromise. It is not a "meeting half-way," not a making of concessions, not a bargain with hostile forces. A compromise can always be expressed or symbolized by figures. A man wants to sell for $5.00, and another wants to buy for $4.00; they will compromise on a price of $4.50. It is the same with all economic affairs, the same with all political treaties. This is compromise.

But there are situations where no compromise is possible. Two people standing at a cross-road have either to part, or to decide for one of the two roads. But they may eventually agree to look out for a third way, the middle road. There is such a road to be found oftener than one would think, if people would only care to look for it.

The success of radicalism is furthered by the idea that by following the middle road man has to give up the pursuit of ideals. This is not true either. The ideals of radicalism are rather uncanny figures; they are so one-sided that they generally exclude others which in truth are quite compatible with the first. The radicals become, accordingly, more or less narrow-minded; it is as if they wore blinkers which allow them to perceive but a very small section of reality.

One need not be a radical for strenuously and persistently pursuing an ideal; one had even better not be. The ideals no more exist in isolation than do real things; the world of ideals is a structure just as complex as the world of reality. No true ideal contradicts absolutely another one. But radicalism excludes all but the one or the few ideals it views. The radical is subjectively an idealist, or at least may be one; but his idealism will remain rudimentary.

There are two extremes one has to avoid when pursuing an ideal. The middle road between these extremes has to be found. Both are equally dangerous. There is the Scylla of unruly self-reliance and the Charybdis of unwarranted self-distrust; one may speak also of the dilemma between exaggerated hopefulness and unreasonable despondency.

Though it is written that God's yoke is light, many people find religious life exceedingly hard. They give up or do not even start because of the difficulties they will have to encounter. Many desist from further endeavors because they do not progress as fast as they imagined they would. Impatience is as great an obstacle here as it is elsewhere. Most people know, however, that they ought to go on; they need, therefore, some excuse for not doing so. One rather popular excuse is found in the idea that there are two kinds of ideals, namely, one for the common man and another for the elect. A perfect religious life is, according to this view, something reserved for some persons who are gifted in a special manner or leading a peculiar life as, for instance, those in holy orders. People holding this view find a confirmation of their ideas in the numerous books on religious life written by monks or nuns for the members of their Orders. It is true that some of these books belong to ages of long ago and that they suppose sometimes an order of life and a world different from those of today. But this cannot invalidate the truth that the goal of Christian life is always and everywhere the same. There is no special ideal for the monk or the priest, no ideal which would be absolutely beyond what every man ought to strive for. Some people may simply ignore this truth; but the majority holds the opposite view just for the sake of silencing the voice of conscience. They are rather like the fox who made himself believe that the grapes were no grapes after all.

This is not the only occasion where to have an excuse ready is very useful indeed. The habit of excusing is a thoroughly bad one. It springs mostly from vanity, from the desire to avoid the unpleasant feeling of having made a mistake or committed a fault. Man wants to appear better than he is in the eyes of the world, but even more in his own. By inventing excuses he tries to fool his conscience in the same manner he is trying to fool his fellows. This habit of excusing every mistake would not be so bad after all, if the goal a man is striving for were really perfection and if his not having attained it were the reason for his making excuses; but this is not the case. These people do not seek perfection for perfection's sake, but for the gratification it affords their vanity; they want to be perfect as they want to wear a nice suit; the attire of their soul has to be as faultless as their tie or their hat or their patent-leather shoes. Those who really aim at perfection do not look around for excuses; they rather register their mistakes because they know them to be inevitable and facts by which they may profit.

Man can not hope for making progress in religious life unless he becomes fully conscious of the mistakes he makes; by hiding them before his own conscience he will never move on. The habit of excusing himself is therefore a real hindrance.

This habit is, however, but one side of a more general attitude—the unwillingness of becoming aware of one's true nature. This unwillingness is in truth itself a sign of something being amiss with our personality. If we were quite sure that we never can detect a serious de-

ficiency, nor any greater imperfection, nor something
basically wrong within ourselves, we surely would
gladly investigate the depths of our personality. That
we shun such an exploration is a sure sign of our knowing dimly that rather unpleasant discoveries await us.

Of some of these painful things we have a more or
less clear idea; of others we just feel that they will be
all but agreeable to face. To the first class belong
many memories of deeds of which we are ashamed or
which we repent of having done; they are not entirely
forgotten, but they have been banished from our every-
day consciousness, and we don't want them to turn up
again. There are, furthermore, many good purposes,
formed once and never carried out or abandoned after
a few attempts; of these too we do not want to be reminded. There is perhaps some undesirable quality
which however manifests itself only occasionally as, for
instance, outbreaks of sudden anger; every time such
an outbreak occurred we resolved that it should be the
last time; but we forget this resolution or rather we do
not follow it up. We know all the time that we ought
to do something, but we do not act according to our
knowledge. From all these things we look away but
too gladly, and we do not like to become aware of them.

Of these things we know sometimes; but there are
others we never really know, though their presence is
not absolutely hidden to us. There is the vanity which
pervades all our actions, the egoism mixed up with our
most unselfish intentions, the pride which will boast
secretly even of humility and sincerity, the ambition
which is never satisfied by any success whatever, the unruly longing for praise, the ingrained tendency for
envy—all those attributes of average human nature
which are the powerful agents of most of our troubles.
Try as we may to convince ourselves that all is right
with us, that we are a quite respectable sort of man,

still, in the depths of our minds we know this to be untrue. And we do not want at all this knowledge to
become really clear. We do all we can to prevent any
light falling into these depths.

This reluctance of becoming aware of our true nature
and the real state of things is a very great, indeed the
greatest, obstacle on the way of religious progress. Many
other undesirable features are but manifestations of this
basic attitude.

The fact of hypocrisy and pharisaism has been
touched upon already. We all behave more or less like
the Pharisee in the Gospel who took pride in his fault-
lessness, telling God how righteously he lived, and how
grateful he was for not being like other people, for instance like the man there behind who just beat his breast
saying: "God have mercy on me, a sinner." We have
to assume this attitude, because it enables us better than
any other to shut the eyes in face of what we in fact
know ourselves to be.

Another feature deriving from this lack of sincerity
is the conviction of not being capable of real progress.
We do not doubt our capacity of becoming better because we know ourselves to be so utterly bad, but because the very first step would lead us into acknowledging that we are far from being as perfect as we make
ourselves believe. The difficulty we recoil from is not
so much the steepness of the way and its length, but
the fact that we have to face the true picture of our
personality.

There are three degrees of vanity. The lowest is
found in a man who looks at himself in the mirror and
admires himself. The next degree is represented by the
behavior of a man who, looking in the mirror, deplores
his ugliness, implying by this that he in fact is entitled
to beauty. But the highest degree of vanity is of a man
who never even goes near a mirror for fear of discover-

ing that he is not as handsome as he believes and wants himself to be.

Despondency and pusillanimity are two dangerous obstacles. They are much more common than is generally known. They are, both of them, children of vanity and ambition. There is a peculiar kind of spiritual ambition, the wish of reaching the heights of religious life, not for the sake of God's glory, but for the sake of gratifying our vanity. St. John of the Cross, in the introductory chapters of his treatise on *The Dark Night*, where he deals with the faults of beginners, has given us a wonderful description of this spiritual ambition; and in a way we never cease to be beginners.

Because man likes so little to do what is really necessary, he often goes off in rather curious bypaths which indeed are truly nonsensical. He acts exactly as it is written, swallowing camels—or having swallowed them already before--and straining at gnats. He is anxiously avoiding even the semblance of sin and imperfection, he is trembling at being eventually caught in one of the many snares besetting his way, he is suspecting sinfulness everywhere and obsessed by the idea that he might have violated some law or that he will do so in the next moment, and he is unaware all the time that something is basically wrong with him. There are certain over-conscientious people whose life is filled with the fear of sins which they may have committed or which they possibly could commit. This state of mind is call scrupulosity. To discuss its nature and origin is out of question; this problem indeed belongs to the pathology of neurosis, since scrupulosity is in truth nothing else but a peculiar form of compulsory neurosis. Only one point has to be made clear: scrupulosity has nothing in common with a real and earnest striving for perfection; it is rather an absolute obstacle to all endeavor of this kind. Scrupulosity is essentially the outcome of a perverted religious life. A person afflicted by this state would do well in reading carefully over the passages Father William Faber devoted to this matter in his treatise, on *Growth in Holiness*. But it is doubtful whether a scrupulous person would be willing to recognize the picture drawn by Father Faber as that of his own personality.

The masters of ascetic theology have always been aware of the fact that scrupulosity is anything but a sign of a really tender conscience. It is the effect of a wrong spiritual ambition combined with cowardice. John Charlier, surnamed De Gerson, and honored by the title of the Very Christian Doctor, who had been chancellor of the University of Paris in the fourteenth century, treated of scrupulosity in a small book entitled *On Pusillanimity*. Many of the men who by profession had to take care of souls, be they priests or alienists, have seen very clearly into this matter; but it is very difficult to make the scrupulous person see what he is really about.

Pusillanimity may manifest itself in other ways too. The catechism mentions a sin called despair of God's mercy. This attitude is commoner than one would think. Even more frequent is another, closely related to the first, namely, the idea that God does not care for one. Many people believe themselves to be what they term God's step-children. Many of these people think that they humbly accept whatever God sends them; but in truth they are not as humble as they believe. For to pass a judgment on God's plans and on the way He is treating us, we must first be able to see through His mind. By feeling like a "step-child" of God man indicates that he in fact knows perfectly how God ought to treat him, that he has quite an inkling of what he deserves and that, accordingly, his mind is equal to penetrating Eternal Wisdom. If man would but care to figure out what the real meaning of this attitude of criticism is, he would become aware of its nonsensicality.

There are quite a few who think and speak as if they wanted to say: "What a pity the Lord did not consult me when he made the world; He would have profited indeed by my advice." Much is of course wrong in this world; but it is not wrong because creation is bad in itself, but because of the wrong use man makes of it. What these critics of Providence find fault with is, however, often not this or that accidental feature of the world but its basic construction. They are quite shocked, for instance, that there are differences between individuals, or between the sexes, or that man must die. They are extremely shocked by the fact that no better place has been allotted to them. They are dissatisfied with everything, grumbling at everything, sure that they would have done much better, had they but been asked.

Not as if a certain kind of dissatisfaction were essentially and always wrong. Dissatisfaction is indeed the great dynamic element pushing mankind forwards. If man had not been dissatisfied with his condition no progress would have been achieved at all. Dissatisfaction and curiosity—which is but a kind of dissatisfaction of the intellect—have been the great forces urging man onwards on the way of discovery and of improvement. Dissatisfaction with himself is the strongest motive starting him on the road to perfection. But this feeling is reasonable and valuable only so long as it deals with sides of reality which are essentially capable of being changed, and it becomes nonsensical when turning on features of reality which must necessarily remain the same.

Fear of death is a natural reaction; but revolt against the fact that man is a mortal animal is nonsensical and indeed wrong. Natural though it is, fear of death— and, for that matter, many kinds of fear—are antagonistic to religious progress. Fear and anxiety may become a kind of obsession filling, as it were, the mind so completely that scarcely any place is left for any other thought.

It is impossible to detail here all that could be and ought to be said on the subject of fear and anxiety. This is so large and important a matter that to discuss it thoroughly a special treatise would become necessary. Only a few things can be pointed out which are immediately related to the question of religious development.

Fear and anxiety are emotions which generally assume a rather egoistic character. Even the fear for another is mostly in truth fear for ourselves. When we fear the death of our beloved we are thinking more of "our loss"—as language very aptly expresses it—than of the person we are in danger of losing. Usually what we fear has a direct bearing on our own welfare; to take care of this is, up to a certain degree, quite right and even a duty. Here as everywhere else it is the passing beyond a limit which becomes wrong.

"The fear of the Lord," say the Scriptures, "is the beginning of wisdom." But it is not more than just the beginning. "The fear of the slave," says St. Bernard, "is the lowest degree of religious mind." "In trembling and in fear," writes St. Paul, "we work our salvation." But the important thing in this is not fear and trembling, but our working our salvation, which means our keeping in mind God's honor and glory. The fears which usually beset human life are mostly of another nature. Even in the fear of death the thought of God's judgment plays but a small rôle; fear of death is much more "natural" than that.

It is not for everyone to feel as St. Francis did. We may not be able to make our own his words: "Praised be Thou, our Lord, for our sister, bodily death." But we may at least try to get a more correct and more rea-

sonable view of death. Did we but fear it, there were
not so much wrong with our attitude. We do, however,
not only fear death; we revolt against it and we feel it
to be a tremendous injustice that we have to die. No
matter how sure we may be of a future life, we nevertheless would prefer this life to go on eternally. In this
feeling there is a good deal of envy too. We have to
depart from this world, and others are allowed to stay
on.

It is this element of rebellion which becomes, not only
in the instance of fear, such an obstacle to religious
progress. Revolt is, of course, the peculiar form in
which the pride of the weak and the helpless asserts itself. Man knows but too well, whether he allows this
thought to become conscious or not, that he is no match
for the great forces governing reality, be it that he calls
them God or destiny or by whatever name. There is a
knowledge so deeply rooted in human nature that one
would really like to think of it as an inborn one, which
tells every soul of its finiteness and smallness and of
something infinitely greater than man. He is forced to
recognize its existence; he may deny it, but it is there
nevertheless. It is too strong for man to resist, too
strong even for his revolting openly against it. He
needs must hide his rebellion before his own consciousness to be able to maintain this attitude. He has to invent, if this expression may pass, some trick enabling
him to keep up the attitude of rebellion without seeming
to do so. One of these tricks, a very powerful one indeed, is the commuting of subjective unwillingness into
an objective impossibility; replacing, that is, the attitude of: "I will not" by the other: "I can not."

There are temptations allegedly so strong that they
can not be resisted; but one has every reason to doubt
the truth of this statement. Perhaps one ought to abstract from certain, indeed abnormal, cases in which

the will may really have become enfeebled as, for instance, in a man addicted to the drug-habit. It is perhaps true that such a man can not resist the temptation any more and has to yield to his craving for the poison. But even in these cases there is a remnant of freedom and a chance for recuperation. It is known that even an inveterate habit of this kind may give way under the pressure of some strong emotion; what emotional strain may produce, will guided by reason ought to be able to accomplish. In fact, there are not a few cases in which a man found the strength to overcome such a habit.

The excuse of chronic intoxication and of bodily changes influencing will does not hold good outside of the cases of toxicomania. The idea of irresistible temptations is probably altogether wrong; great as the alluring force may be, it still needs the assent of the will for man to give way to it. But we do, in fact, cede very often to temptations which we can not, in good conscience, credit with an overwhelming power. Why does man yield so easily to temptation?

The answer has been given, once and for ever, by St. Augustine in an exceedingly interesting passage of his *Confessions,* where he tells of his having stolen, when a boy, fruits from the neighbor's orchard. He did not eat those fruits; those he had at home were better than the stolen ones. What attracted him was not the spoil to be got, but the stealing itself. There is indeed a peculiar fascination in doing things forbidden; an old adage asserts that we always strive for the things forbidden and long for those denied to us. The fact is well known; St. Augustine supplies the explanation. By trespassing, by ignoring a commandment, by consciously acting in contradiction to what we know to be the law, man gives to himself the illusion of being greater than the law-giving power; he gives himself for a moment a feeling of superiority and even, when the commandment ignored be of Divine origin, the illusion of being more than God Himself. It is as if the words of the serpent were still resounding in man's ears: "You will be like gods. . . ."

The self-willed and self-asserting ego shrinks from the idea of submitting whole-heartedly to the will of God. The devil takes, it is said, the hand when he is offered a finger; but God is sure to take the whole man. And where will our precious self be when the Almighty gets hold of it; how to assert our self, when it has but to do God's will; and will not such a total surrender simply abolish our personality and turn its freedom and dignity into bondage and slavery? We do not, as a rule, ask these questions, because they are contrary to what we have been taught. But we oftener than not behave as if such ideas were in our mind. If they are—and there is no doubt of it—they are to a large extent the outcome of ignorance and misunderstanding. We simply do not know enough, either of reality, or of God, or of ourselves.

After all there is but reason and knowledge to show us the way. It is not in vain that the Scriptures say that we shall know the truth and truth shall make us free.

The ideas on freedom held by many people are, however, often very far from the one implied in the words of the Gospel, and the ideas on truth are not less so. Faith teaches man that truth is to be found in revelation and in the ordinances of the Church, and that freedom consists in the assent given to truth as well as in the determination to act according to it. But the human mind confuses very easily objective truth with ideas it can completely understand and which it can find out by itself, and believes that freedom is to be had only in lawlessness or, at least, where the laws are of man's own making. Here again one is strongly reminded of the treacherous promises made by the serpent: "You will be like gods"; being like gods means having nothing above onself, being the absolute master of one's fate, the supreme power within reality; knowing about good and evil means that the laws ruling over human behavior shall be made by man himself, that he shall decree what is permitted and what forbidden.

The difficulties which belong in a special sense to religious life, the resistance some people feel against obeying this or that commandment can not be detailed here. Some general remarks, however, on the psychological side of these difficulties and on the basic features of unbelief have to be mentioned. Faith is, according to the teachings of the Church, due to Divine grace. It is more than a mere believing in statements. But supernatural though faith is in its essence, it is not without a natural aspect too; grace supposes nature, and this statement of theology implies that a certain collaboration and a certain readiness for listening to the voice of grace has to be prepared by the human mind to become capable of being enlighted by the rays of revelation. Once in an address delivered to a meeting on Religious Psychology a man, equally famous as a priest, a scholar and a statesman, remarked that there is no psychology of faith, in the strict sense of the terms, faith being essentially of a supernatural origin, but that psychology may well inquire into the essence of unbelief, since this attitude is due to the natural factors influencing human mind. The same may be said of certain difficulties that people who want to believe and to adhere to their faith encounter in religious life.

Faith means the acceptance of articles which rest on the authority of Revelation, of the Scriptures, of the Church. Believing in authority means submission to it.

Rejection of authority is always something like rebellion, at least it is born out of the desire for self-assertion.

Many people feel that they can not believe what they can not understand; they are utterly wrong in this, because one can not believe and need not believe what reason is capable of proving. We do not believe in mathematics; we knows its statements to be true, because we can prove them, demonstrate them and make everyone see that they are true. There are, of course, many things we believe, insofar as we are not able to verify them. The layman believes what the scientist or the historian tells him, not having the possibility of inquiring by himself into all these things. We believe what a traveler tells us about a foreign country, because we have no means of going there and seeing with our own eyes. But in all these cases there is the chance of verification; had we studied physics, read the original documents, gone to the foreign countries, we could ascertain whether the reports and statements are true or not. We see, therefore, no great difficulty in believing these people, unless they tell us things we deem to be altogether improbable. But with faith it is different; nobody can expect to get a verification of the articles of faith; we have simply to believe them.

The human mind does not, in fact, find this belief too difficult; there have been at all times and there are today many very clever men, many who are fully acquainted with the principles of science, many thoroughly capable of handling the methods of science and of logic, who readily believe what faith and the Church teach. Believing in these things is evidently not at all contrary to reason. The articles of faith are indeed not against reason, though they transcend it. An unprejudiced and clear-headed philosophy may even push its inquiries up to a point where the answer given by faith appears as the most plausible one, though philosophy can never really prove it. It is not reason which induces man to reject faith or to doubt its truth.

The great anti-religious movements started with what they called "humanism." This term is used in many senses; but it implies always that man is made the centre of the universe, the pivot, as it were, on which all the rest turns. It is rather noteworthy that the French Revolution, whose anti-Christian attitude is generally known, proclaimed solemnly the "rights of man." These rights were, in truth, quite sufficiently safeguarded by Christian religion; they needed not to be stated anew; they were not at all discovered in those bloody times. Their being stated expressly by the spiritual leaders of the French Revolution is significant, however, of the general mentality: man was to be made the absolute centre of the world. The revolution of that time, and the same may be asserted of every revolution afterwards, turned not only against the social order, against the supremacy of certain classes, against the existing structure of society and the economic situation resulting therefrom; it turned against every order and authority which was not acknowledgedly of man's making. Though the economic distress of a large majority of the people played manifestly the greatest rôle in the origins of the Revolution, the unwillingness of accepting an established order, which moreover appealed to Divine institution, was a very mighty factor in preparing the revolutionary attitude.

The war waged by all kinds of revolutionaries, of free-thinkers, of "progressive" and "enlightened" people against religion is declared, nearly without any exception, in the name of "reason." But reason, since it can not give an all-convincing proof that the articles of faith are true, can not disprove them either. Science, especially, has no means of criticising religious statements. It is not man's reason but man's pride which revolts against faith. This very pride which once, even before man yielded to the insinuations of the serpent, had spoken: "I refuse to serve."

What is true of the great anti-religious movements in history is true also of the anti-religious attitude of single individuals. It is not reason which hinders them in accepting the teachings of the Church; they know or are, at least, able to discover, that reason can not bring forth any valid argument against faith; they know that, so far as reason goes, it does not encounter insurmountable obstacles on its way to faith. But pride does; pride is reluctant to accept statements based on authority, even be it the one of Revelation. Pride especially does not want to submit to commandments which it feels to come from without and which it has not been asked to approve previously. So deeply rooted is this pride that it does not even listen to the voice of reason which is quite ready to accept statements it can not prove; reason, in fact, knows perfectly that there are many things it simply has to accept without being able to prove them or to discover why they are at all and why they are just thus. That there is a world and that it is ordered according to laws, that these laws are such as they are, all these things have to be accepted by human reason which never can hope to penetrate the essence of reality. Science discovers these laws, but it is quite incapable of telling us why they are and why they are just thus. The acknowledgment of the laws ruling over nature is indeed forced on the human mind; if these laws were not recognized, man would have to pay the penalty. Things will fall down, whether man is willing to recognize the law of gravity or not; things will hurt us if we do not keep out of their way, regardless of our assenting to the laws. Whether we understand the hidden essence of things or not, they will go on behaving as they did since times unthinkable. Reason knows this, and it knows too that there are other laws which command no less respect than do those of nature. Reason knows that there are the laws of morals, it knows that there must be a ruling principle and an ultimate cause of things and events. It is not reason which recoils from accepting these laws nor from believing in truth revealed. It is pride which bars the way.

Quite a few people who stay outside the faith tell us that they are quite content with accepting the teachings of the Church, but that they can not bring themselves to believe in this or that special article or consent to this or that special ordinance. They think that these objections are dictated by reason. But reason ought to convince them that the teachings of the Church are of an irreproachable logic, and that to accept the premises makes inevitable the acceptance of every conclusion. The non-acceptance of certain single statements results either from an incomplete understanding or from an unwillingness which uses the apparent difficulties of reason for its ends and for remaining hidden from the eyes of the person himself.

Also the doubts by which some believers feel assailed have generally no other cause but the resentment experienced by unruly pride against having to submit to authority or to accept statements reason can not thoroughly penetrate.

PART III

HOW TO HELP ONESELF

1. What to Know

In the foregoing chapters many of the faults giving rise to all kinds of difficulties and troubles or handicapping progress have been described and analyzed. The descriptions are far from being exhaustive; much more could be said on the single attitudes and features of behavior, and there are many things which have not even been mentioned. What has been said is, however, notwithstanding this incompleteness, probably sufficient for a man to become aware of the many snares awaiting him on his way and the many self-deceptions barring it.

It is surely something, it is even quite a deal to know about these pitfalls and dangers. To avoid the ones and to overcome the others we have first to be fully aware of them. But this knowledge of the dangers which surround us does not as yet enable a man to go his way; such a knowledge may even have quite the opposite effect, namely, of discouraging a man, of making him feel incapable of the task set before him, and it may thus bring him to a standstill. Knowledge being doubtless the first step on the way of progress is evidently not more than just a beginning.

The help to be gained from knowledge is, however, greater than is generally believed. By becoming aware of the nature of the real difficulties in which we are entangled we discover new sides in them and thus new chances of dealing with them. Knowledge often opens suddenly an altogether new way, one we never thought of before, giving access to a place which we before despaired of ever reaching.

But a man may set out, full of hope, to climb the newly discovered path and he may suffer disappointment. The path is neither as short nor as easy as he thought. There are many ups and downs, many detours; there are abysses to be skirted, stumbling-blocks to be avoided, steep slopes to be climbed; the man toils on and on, but the summit seems to be as far away as it had been when he started. Fatigue and disillusion befall him; his ascent becomes gradually slower, finally he begins to glide back, and before long he finds himself at the spot from which he started.

One needs more to climb a mountain than the mere knowledge of the route to follow. Nobody can hope to reach the summit without having acquired a certain technique and having undergone a certain training.

Technique and training can not be acquired from books. They need, besides the theoretical knowledge, a good deal of practice. The words of Aristotle on acquiring a virtue have been already quoted; they contain a very important truth. A virtue can be acquired only by exercising it. There are, however, quite a few who find this advice very objectionable. Practising appears to them to be all right so long as we have to acquire some capacity or to train for some work. But they hold this to be wrong and even immoral, in the case of attempting to acquire a virtue; a man practising a virtue which he has not really got, they say, becomes guilty of hypocrisy; he is simply assuming a moral character he in fact does not have.

If this were true there would be no chance at all of ever making progress, unless it were by an extraordinary intervention of Divine grace. The objection mentioned seems to spring from a very tender conscience; but it is really either the result of a very confused idea of what hypocrisy is, or just an apparently forcible and convincing reason for doing nothing.

By the name of hypocrisy is called the behavior of a person who wants to create the impression of being honest, moral, pious, etc., for the sake of some egoistical aims; maybe he wants to be honored as a perfect citizen, maybe he wants to get some position, maybe he wants to impose on other people for some criminal purpose, maybe he simply wants to gratify his vanity. The essential feature in hypocrisy is that a moral behavior is assumed not because of its being intrinsically good, but because of some other reasons. The hypocrite generally knows that he is playing a rôle; his picture has been immortalized by Molière in his "Tartuffe." But there is also an unconscious hypocrisy in people who believe themselves to be most perfect, while they have, in truth, only the outward behavior of morality and are, in the depths of their souls, callous and egoistical; that is what is called rightly by the name of pharisaism. These people know all about the laws of morality; they are the severest judges of their neighbors; they are shocked by the slightest infringement of ethics, provided it is committed by others; they are prudish and priggish and supercilious—but all this is only façade, behind which dwell things wholly different.

To strive for the good because of its goodness, to do the right things because of their being right, to behave in the way prescribed by morality because it is the moral way, is in truth the very opposite of hypocrisy. The mistaken idea which is criticized here arises from an erroneous conception of the importance of certain subjective states of mind. Not everyone can be expected, nor can he expect himself, to feel in the way he knows to be the right one. We may very well be willing to do certain things and to do them really and at the same time not feel like doing them; many things are done reluctantly. But the point is not whether a man feels like doing this or that, but whether he does it or not. By acting according to the laws of morality man shows that he is willing to respect these laws and to acknowledge their binding power. It is much if a man acts regularly in this manner; his feelings are only of a secondary importance.

An action which is right in itself does not become less so, nor are its results and its influence on the doer's personality weakened by the fact that it is not associated with enthusiasm and feeling. It is, of course, more pleasant to do things one feels enthusiastic about than those which necessitate an overcoming of reluctance. An action of the second type may be perhaps more meritorious. But the merit of an action does not depend on the amount of reluctance which had to be surmounted.

It is, of course, not for this book to discuss the theological side of the question of sacrifice, still less the problem of its merits. But the psychological side of this problem must be touched upon by a few remarks.

First of all, there is a certain prejudice against sacrifice. This prejudice is found not only with persons who deny the value and the need of sacrifice—because they profess some egoistical kind of philosophy—but also with people who know very well that there is a need of sacrifice and that by making sacrifices they are acquiring merit and obeying the laws of morals and of religion. According to this idea sacrifice comes to be regarded as something "unnatural," as something alien to the laws and the essence of life, something like a yoke to be born by mankind. The enemies of Christian morality and the advocates of "natural" life (by which name they usually mean a life addicted to pleasure and to gaining as much satisfaction of human desire as possible) make much of this argument which in truth has no strength whatever.

Sacrifice in the full sense of the word does not indeed appear on a level of existence lower than that of man. True sacrifice presupposes reason and free will. But facts which present a rather striking analogy to sacrifice may be observed already in infra-human levels. The essence of sacrifice consists in giving away something valuable for the sake of realizing a still higher value. If a man deprives himself of some pleasure and prefers to spend the money for charity, he is making a sacrifice; pleasure means something to him, it has a definite value, but he understands that an act of charity represents objectively a much higher value and he is willing to realize this value, though the giving up of pleasure is felt to be rather disagreeable. If, however, pleasure had no allurement for this man, his giving money to charity would still be, of course, a charitable act, but there would be no sacrifice.

Every kind of becoming or of evolution causes some value to disappear, to be destroyed, or to be not realized. The values connected with childhood disappear when the child grows to be a man. It is evident—and mothers feel this most strongly—that the gradual disappearance of all the charming features characteristic of childhood means a real destruction of values; something disappears which has a definite value not only in the eyes of the loving mother but in an objective sense too. A raw diamond is cut and polished; from this a stone results whose value is much greater than that of the raw stone; but the original size has become diminished and parts of it are lost altogether.

The disappearance of certain values for the sake of the realization of others, higher ones, is probably due to a general law of reality. It does not make any difference whether this realization is brought about by the forces of nature, as in the growth of the child, or by the cunning of man. No value can become real unless another value, of a lesser rank, is destroyed.

Sacrifice, therefore, is not at all "unnatural"; it is rather the manifestation of this general law within the level of human existence. Denying the sense, the value, and the necessity of sacrifice amounts to denying the peculiarity and dignity of human nature. By taking this point of view the adversaries of Christian morals do not, as they believe, defend the rights of human nature; they are rather dragging down this nature to the level of mere animal life.

All people agree that sacrifice remains what it is and retains its specific value, whether one feels enthusiastic about it or not. The emotional background is not an essential part of sacrifice, as it is indeed of no action whatsoever. Action consists in the adoption of the conclusions reason proposes and in realizing the aims resulting from these considerations. The objective truth on which an action is based and the objective values it strives to realize are the only things which matter; feeling is but an accessory factor.

A person, therefore, acting in the line of virtue without possessing already this virtue to its full extent and not reacting emotionally as he would wish to do, does not become guilty of hypocrisy. He would become so only if he were satisfied with making believe and if he did not really want to acquire this virtue.

There is no truth not liable to misinterpretation and misuse. This holds good also for the idea of sacrifice. An astonishingly large number of people believe that by doing something disagreeable they are making a sacrifice and, accordingly, acquiring merit. The question of merit is not one this book can consider. Maybe there is some merit, even in a rather nonsensical action so long as there is a really good intention. There are, however, people who will take on themselves really great troubles, real sufferings, and who are, nevertheless, unaware of their neglecting some very obvious and important duties. They deny to themselves, for instance, some innocent pleasure; they are intent on procuring some very unpleasant sensations—for instance, putting a lot of salt in their soup—and they do not realize at all that they are lacking in true love for their neighbors.

There are so many opportunities for making sacrifices which are to some good, by which we may help other people, or contribute a little to alleviate sufferings, that we really need not turn to such more or less nonsensical actions. There will be enough time to turn to eating disgusting things or to sleep on broken nut-shells when all other sacrifices we possibly can make are done with. But it is doubtful whether an average person—we leave out the saints—will ever arrive at this point.

It is not enough to be resolved to make sacrifices; one must know what sacrifices are indicated. Here as always the first question to be asked is: where to begin. In regard to the improvement of ourselves or of progress a general answer is clear from the very outset. There are two ways: one starting at the centre of personality and proceeding towards the periphery, and a second one starting from without or from the outward manifestations and penetrating gradually into the core of personality.

In the first case we have to attempt to change the very basic attitudes and ideas which, consciously or not, regulate our behavior. In the second case we have to try to influence these underlying attitudes by transforming our habits step by step.

It has been explained already that the faults a man commits, the troubles he gets into, the difficulties harrassing him, have their origin in the very depths of his personality, that they spring from or are expressions of certain deeply buried but exceedingly powerful tendencies of human nature. The first way of procedure, the attempt to reform and to remould personality from within, seems therefore to be the best and indeed the only way. This idea is theoretically quite right. But things present a somehow different aspect from the point of view of practice. The access to the depths of personality is often not so easy that we could think of working immediately on the basic attitudes of the ego. Even if we have discovered what these fundamental attitudes are like, even if we have become sure that unruly pride, exaggerated self-love, uncommon vanity, or cowardly ambition are at the bottom of all our difficulties; even if all this is perfectly clear to us, even if we know what we ought to do, we still may be quite incapable of translating, as it were, this knowledge into efficient actions. Though we may know what is amiss with ourselves and what changes have to be brought about, we may be as helpless in face of this task as we ever had been before.

There is a very hard, though diaphanous shell around the centre of our personality. Once we have torn away the veil which forbade a clear vision of the depths of the ego, we may see quite clearly what is lurking inside this shell; it may indeed become clear as a crystal, but it is also not less hard. Our knowledge penetrates far deeper into ourself than does our will. We see the monsters of the deep, we may shudder at their aspect, but we cannot break through the shell to kill them.

In some rare cases indeed the shell may burst open under the tension from within or the pressure from without; man can become suddenly changed by a real conversion or be forced to change by circumstances. Such cases are, however, exceptions. As a rule man has patiently and persistently to work on the shell so as to make it slowly thinner until his will can break through.

Neither is the task of getting a clear vision of what is contained in this shell an easy one. Rarely are we given such an insight all of a sudden; generally the knowledge of the basic attitudes develops only gradually. Happily we need not wait until this vision has become complete and perfectly clear. If we had, this would be very bad indeed. The knowledge of our self is never really completed; we may believe we know all about ourselves and we may, nevertheless, suddenly discover things of whose existence we were wholly unaware. The discovery of the self can not be likened to the determining of the geographical position of some lonely island, lost amidst the sea. The geographer's task is done, in this case, once he has figured out the exact latitude and longitude. Discovering the self is more like drawing a complete map of some richly structured country. One gets first a general survey, for instance, by a photography taken from an airplane; this picture being on a small scale, shows that there is a river at one place and a farm at another, that there are some hills and that parts of the land look swampy. A larger map has to be drawn on which all the little brooks will have to be represented and the roads and the bridges, the houses and the barns. A third map, still larger, shows noticeable trees and the crosses on the wayside or a little chapel somewhere on a hill, it shows too where farmer Jones' land ends and neighbor Smith's acres begin. This map is a real help to the wanderer, since he can gather from it that he may shorten his way by walking straight on to this or that tree instead of following the sinuosities of the road. But even this map does not supply a real knowledge of the country. The people who dwell on this bit of earth and who know it, as it were, by heart, have quite another kind of knowledge. Jones may tell his neighbor that his car got stuck in the hole on the way to the stony acre, and Smith will not only know all about the spot, but he will also know for sure that this hole has become, and in what way it did, more dangerous since the last great rainfall. This is really knowing the land. Such a knowledge is not got by studying a map however large, nor by an occasional visit and by strolling over the ground. To know things in this manner one must live there, must have lived there. And even then, after having been there a life-time, things may turn up which had been hidden until this very moment. Some day, perhaps, Smith will cut down a hedge and find an old and rusty gun which had been thrown away years and years ago, maybe in the Civil War, and of whose existence nobody knew. Or he may cut down a tree and dig out its stump and come on a skeleton with a fractured skull; and when he tells of his discovery an old woman will remark that she remembers her grandmother mentioning the disap-pearance of a farm-hand at the time when she was still a little girl.

We may live a lifetime on the land of our own soul and still remain ignorant of many details. Every day may bring a new and astounding discovery. There may be old and forgotten things which have fallen into de-cay. Sometimes we just look at them without being able to locate them. But sometimes also a dim light dawns on us and we remember things of long ago, things which had been brand new then and which we could have used perhaps, had we but paid attention to them. We too, like the man who lost his rifle, throw away things we could have used, and we too discover skeletons telling of awful deeds which did not appear so horrid at the time they were perpetrated.

Self-knowledge, therefore, is never completed; the careful search for hidden motives, for egoistical tendencies masquerading as the purest altruism or appearing as the inevitable results of circumstances, for unruly self-assertion going crooked ways, since it dares not show in the open; the hunt for all this can never be given up. But we have not, let this be said once more, to wait until this search is at its end; we can, we are even obliged to start the work of reconstruction immediately after having made our first discoveries. A country full of swamps is indeed won thoroughly for cultural ends only after all the swamps have been dried up; but one can begin to sow after the first few acres have been turned into fertile soil. It is the same with personality. Unveiling some nefarious tendency, breaking into its hiding place, gives a foothold for progress and provides a spot, however small, to build upon.

This search for the truth about ourselves and the attempt of unveiling the hidden egoistical tendencies have some dangers of their own. They too may become masks of egoism and vanity. Instead of pursuing his task for the sake of truth and of an objective good—the perfection of personality being such a good—man may go on hunting for faults merely to gratify his vanity or to find some plausible excuse for his not making progress. There are some who declare that they cannot even think of improvement, since they have as yet a very incomplete idea of themselves. There are others who boast of a very thorough knowledge of their own personality; but who become so enthralled by and so interested in the study of their own precious ego that they forget the real goal and strive for self-knowledge for its own sake. There is a third group of persons who discover such an amount of vanity, so many bad motives, so great an influence of self-assertion in all their actions that they really do not feel like doing anything; they can not do one really good deed; whatever they do, it is bad. By being charitable they are serving their vanity, therefore they refrain from helping other people; by listening to another they are humoring their curiosity, therefore they prefer to do the talking themselves; by doing conscientiously their work they are but feeding their pride, therefore they neglect their duties.

Self-knowledge, or laboring for it, may thus become very dangerous. Here again one must know about the middle way and keep to it. It is as wrong to develop an undue interest in one's own personality as it is not to care for it at all. There is only, as it seems, one kind of motive which will make us hold to the middle way: that to be found in faith. Religion alone teaches man that he has to seek perfection not for his own egoistical ends, but for the glory of God. Having his eyes riveted on this primary aim, man can avoid being caught in the snares menacing his way of progress.

These snares are, in truth, quite dangerous. The knowledge psychology supplies of the many forms which hidden pride, deeply buried ambition, or the will of self-assertion may assume has often a definitely destructive influence. By becoming acquainted with these theories a man may learn to distrust even his clearest impressions or ideas. He develops an inclination to interpret all his thoughts and actions according to these theories of psychology; he becomes incapable of naïve and unsophisticated experience; whatever he thinks or feels or does needs must have some deeper signification, there must be something quite different hidden behind or beneath. Widely though the various schools of psychology differ in their theories, they nevertheless are agreed that mental phenomena may have a significance different from the one they present to immediate experience. But psychology does not say that this is the rule; psychology only warns us that this might be the case. The generalization which makes some people look for a hidden meaning is not the fault of psychology, but the result of a misuse and a misunderstanding of its findings.

Man is right in being suspicious of his motives, especially when he finds an excuse or some apparently moral reason for actions which are either wrong in themselves or whose results prove to be painful for others. But we ought to know that the moral value of an action depends first on the objective value realized by it. It is indeed but too evident that bad, or at least objectionable motives will be mixed up with those prompting us to an even moral action. We are apt to gratify our vanity in being charitable or to feel proud because of our having resisted temptation. But there are many ways of gratifying vanity and many opportunities for feeling proud. Instead of deploring the fact that our charity was not born of an unadulterated love for our neighbor, let us be grateful that it was not merely vanity which made us act in this manner.

A close examination of our motives will, there is no doubt of that, reveal an amazing amount of egoism. The analyses sketched out in the foregoing chapters have shown that an exaggerated love of ourselves and an all too great lack of love of our neighbors, an unruly pride and a very poorly developed humility, an overstrung ambition and a hardly less marked cowardice, a greediness for sensational experience and an unwillingness to accept the place allotted to us, a craving for omnipotence and a reluctance to submit to the laws of reality, that—to summarize all this in one word—the predominance of our ego and our declining to notice this fact are the most powerful and the most frequent reasons of our manifold troubles and difficulties.

We must destroy the roots of an evil to be sure that we have really gained a victory. A complete and lasting victory is not to be hoped for. The evil springs from the very essence of our nature; we can not radically change this nature. It is therefore always possible, even probable, that the evil will return. But if we have become watchful and have learned how to discover it in its initial states, we will be able to deal with it better than we did before. Benjamin Franklin remarks somewhere in his *Autobiography* that he could not boast of having become really humble, though he acquired perfectly the behavior of humility. "Had I become humble," says he, "I probably would have been proud once more, because of my humility."

The influence of an evil can, of course, be lessened or even be abolished, at least temporarily, by more superficial and provisionary means. In medicine there is a distinction of what is called causal and symptomatic treatment. The first name means a method based on the knowledge of the ultimate causes of some disease and attacking directly these causes; malaria is, for example, due to the presence of certain micro-organisms in the blood and these germs are destroyed by quinine. Symptomatic treatment means the appliance of some agent which causes certain symptoms to disappear without acting directly on their causes; for instance, the use of drugs which alleviate pain or produce a fall of abnormally high body-temperature. The causal method is doubtless more efficient, and it corresponds to the ideal. Symptomatic treatment is often inefficient because it leaves untouched the reasons of the pathological state. It becomes important, however, in all cases where some symptom imperils life or gives rise to great subjective sufferings. There are, furthermore, certain conditions by which a vicious circle becomes established of the sort that the pathological process underlying the whole disease is re-inforced by the very symptoms resulting from it. To choose a very simple instance: heart palpitations give rise to a feeling of anxiety and oppression, but these emotions, on the other hand, tend to produce an acceleration of the heart rate.

There is a causal and a symptomatic way of procedure also in regard to the troubles of behavior and of moral life. Here too the symptomatic method very often proves of no avail. This fact is generally known. Nearly everybody remembers the many efforts he has made to overcome this or that habit and of their having been altogether fruitless.

It is, for instance, very often useless to attempt not being untidy any more or not being given to fits of despondency, so long as the roots of these habits remain within ourselves. This does not, however, amount to a license for keeping our faults and for not doing anything against them. We have, even if we do not see any results coming from our endeavors, to go on trying to get rid of these faults or, at least, to prevent their further growth. The apparently fruitless pains and efforts will prove very useful afterwards. When the basic attitudes have been reformed, or, rather, when we begin reforming them, this training in opposing faulty habits will become a very great help. A habit, once established, does not disappear at a moment's notice, even after the attitudes conditioning it have been uprooted. There is a certain *vis inertiae* in us which causes habits to go on. It is more or less a phenomenon like one we very often see in a machine; even after the current driving a motor has been switched off, the wheel will go on turning, because the impulse it has been given does not spend itself all of a sudden.

The vicious circle which has been mentioned before as a phenomenon of pathology, namely, the mutual reinforcement of symptoms and their causes, is a common occurrence in behavior troubles. Wrong attitudes give rise to undesirable habits, and these habits contribute to increase and fortify these attitudes. The process of rebuilding moves along a circle but in the opposite sense. Discouragement lessens the energy of action, which proves accordingly inefficient; the result is failure and failure means a deepening of discouragement. When, on the other hand, a man learns that failure is not an equivalent to defeat, that it is inevitable, that all progress is by "trial and error" and that, therefore, he can not expect his doings to be successful the first time, and that, furthermore, having achieved a little progress is already success or a step towards it, when he has come to change his attitude towards these facts, he will support failure much better; the depression which used to be conditioned by failure will become less or it will disappear altogether and his courage will be strengthened instead of being diminished.

In judging their chances for overcoming some habit or getting rid of some fault people generally make one great mistake. They lay much more stress on failure than on success. They complain that in so many cases they have been unable to avoid falling back into their habit, though they concede that sometimes they happened to be victorious in their struggle against it. We have, however, to bear in mind that the positive facts have always a much greater importance than the negative instances. Instead of pointing exclusively to them, of remembering only the failures, we ought to take account of the moments of success, however rare they may have been. There is every reason to hope that we shall be able to achieve again what has been achieved already once or twice; every success increases the chance of its being repeated, if only we take care to look at things from the right angle.

One has, of course, to avoid the opposite error—the hasty conclusion which considers a first success as a sure sign of a lasting victory. Whoever would indulge in this belief is bound to be disappointed. This unwarranted optimism is however less frequent than its opposite.

Discouragement sets in much too easily. After a few failures many despair of success. They are not sufficiently conscious of the enormous complexity of human affairs. A chemist seeking to synthesize some new compound knows that he is in for a couple of years; his experiments may fail several hundreds of times; he will be very glad if he achieves the synthesis after having failed six hundred times. Human life, individual and social, is much more difficult to handle than the things in a chemical laboratory. The chemist may change at his will the temperature and the time and the concentration and the acidity and any other factors; he is acquainted with almost every factor influencing the process and is able to alter it. But a man desiring to rebuild his life and his personality does not know in the same way the factors determining his experiences and reactions; and those he knows are not to be arranged and influenced as easily. We ought, therefore, to be much more patient than the chemist is. But we do not take account of these facts, and give up generally after having met failure. We say, indeed, that we did try "a thousand times"; but this is never true, not even as a rough approximation. The reason why we give up so soon is, of course, lack of courage; but vanity too plays a great rôle therein; we believe we are entitled to a quick and thoroughgoing success the very moment we condescend to do anything at all.

When starting on the way of progress and improvement we have to be prepared for a lengthy period of unceasing endeavor, for plenty of relapses and failures. But there is, painfully as this need is felt, one great compensation. In things moral and religious earnest striving, conscientious work, honest attempts have a definite value in themselves independent of the success achieved.

In economic life it is only real achievement which counts, and it is much the same with social life; in both cases it is important to have reached a goal. But in the field of morality it is different; there the movement towards a goal is not without merits, if only it is really honest.

This is indeed a great consolation; even the altogether fruitless attempts are not deprived of sense, though they do not lead up to success. Man, however, wants more than consolation for his failures; he wants, and he is quite right in this, to learn how to avoid them.

A religious person will indeed find much help and comfort in prayer. God may answer and help him who earnestly seeks His help. Man left alone is powerless; unless God succors the weakness of human nature, nothing good can be achieved. "We have to know," said St. Ignatius of Loyola, "that in truth nothing depends on us, but we have to act as if all depended on ourselves." We have to be, according to the Epistle of St. James, not only hearers but also doers of God's word. Once a simple Arab, having come from the desert to Mecca, accosted the prophet Mohammed: "Tell me, prophet," he said, "since you are bound to know; ought I to bind my camel or may I trust in God and let the beast run free?" And the prophet replied: "First you bind your camel, and then you trust in God." Even though man can achieve nothing without the help of Divine grace, he must do his part, however small it may be.

The usual idea is that we ought to suppress all undesirable habits, to oppose all tendencies giving rise to difficulties, to refrain from all actions contrary to the laws of society or of morals. But this method is apt to end in failure.

The attempt of merely suppressing or opposing what we feel to be wrong is not successful because it is of a purely negative nature. If we tell a man that he need not pay attention to this or to that without pointing out to him some other thing he may turn his eyes to, we put him to an indeed very difficult task. He has to find out by himself where to turn his attention, and he is likely not to find anything captivating his interest, since he is interested just in the thing forbidden to him. The fact of being prohibited to look in a certain direction is, furthermore, quite a strong incentive to do so. The chance of his obeying will be rather small unless we provide something sufficiently interesting. The attraction of things forbidden has its root, of course, in the unwillingness to submit to restrictions. This is a well-known topic of many fairy-tales all over the world: you may open all the doors, but the one which the little golden key fits you must not open.

Positive rules or commands are generally more efficient than prohibitive measures. A person desiring to lose certain habits and to acquire new and better ones will profit more by considering the positive aspect of the laws to be obeyed.

These laws are very often misunderstood. Man tends, by his very nature, to please himself and to rebel against the laws of reality and of morals. He is not aware of the fact that this rebellion turns as much against himself as against reality. Man conceives these laws which tend to curb his own stubborn pride as something alien to his person, something outside of the ego, something emanating from a region to which man has no access and to which he does not belong. He feels as if he were outside of the world, as if it depended on his free will to join reality or not. He knows, of course, that he cannot dispense altogether with reality, but he believes that he can restrict his contact with reality just to the minimum he is pleased to concede. Man can create for himself the illusion that he is free to acknowledge reality or to reject it; he never can, in truth, get outside of it.

He is, willingly or not, a member or an element of this very reality from the first moment of his existence to his last. He cannot even imagine himself as existing without a reality surrounding him and to which he belongs. The mistaken idea, as if reality and the human person were two things which come together only accidentally, is fed on certain phrases, very commonly used, but wrong nevertheless; phrases like these: "the individual and society," "the ego and the world." These antitheses seem to imply an absolute opposition of the two terms. But the individual does not exist independently of and isolated from society; human personality develops only within society. It is impossible to imagine a human being absolutely alone; without the contact with others there is neither speech nor thought, nor character, nor morals. Man is necessarily a member of society and an element of reality. The laws governing reality—in the largest sense of the word—are accordingly also the laws of individual existence. Though these laws may sometimes appear as alien or strange or even hostile, they are in truth the very basis of each individual's existence. By revolting, therefore, against the laws of reality, man wages war against his very own existence; the very personal being of a person becomes endangered by its unwillingness to accept the laws of reality and to submit to them. This is the reason why maladjustment to reality leads inevitably to conflicts within personality itself.

The same reflections apply to morals. Morality is the sum-total of all laws related to the order of values. Values are not vague notions, floating as it were in an empty space, and they are not mere subjective states or feelings. They are a very definite side of reality; every being, says philosophy, is one and true and good; goodness or value is as much a feature of reality as any other we credit things with. Maladjustment to the moral laws is, therefore, as disastrous to personality as is the non-adaptation to what is generally understood by the term of reality.

This point must be well understood. No real progress and no improvement can be hoped for, unless man is fully aware of this: that by submitting to the laws of reality and those of morals and by regulating his behavior as far as possible according to them, he is not only obeying forces which resent and punish disobedience very hard, but that he is, at the same time, serving by this himself and his own ends. By revolting against these laws and by making the indeed futile attempt to escape from them he is undermining the very basis of his own existence.

The essence of a law is always an assertion. The law may, it is true, be expressed in a negative form, but it is essentially positive by its nature. Some of the ten commandments, for instance, are couched in a negative form: thou shalt not. So are often the definitions and ordinances of the Church. But we are taught by Christ Himself that the essence of the law is a positive one, when He says that the two great commandments, of the love of God and the love of our neighbor, contain the whole law and all the prophets.

The meaning of the laws expressed by a negative formula is undoubtedly a positive one. The commandment which forbids theft enjoins in fact the respect for another's property. The commandment forbidding murder teaches the sacredness of human life. Human nature being what it is, a formula enjoining respect for property or preaching the sacredness of human life would be probably much less efficient than the solemn: thou shalt not. Eternal Wisdom saw fit to choose the negative form, because it is more impressive and because God, in His mercy, enunciated to His people just the minimum of duties. Avoidance of things forbidden is indeed but the indispensable minimum of moral life; it is just a platform from which to start.

It has been pointed out repeatedly that recognizing the objective order of value is of an absolutely decisive importance in self-improvement. A mere theoretical knowledge, however, is not sufficient. Even before we proceed to apply our knowledge to the regulation of our actions, we must develop within ourselves the attitude of respect or reverence, as the one which alone is due to the order of values. We have to admire only what is really worth being admired, we must learn to be enthusiastic only about what really deserves such a reaction. On the other hand we have to know that every bit of reality is endowed with some value and that reality contains nothing which would be totally deprived of value.

This awareness of values and their order is just what is aptly called reverence. This state of mind has become unhappily rather rare in modern times. It is not for these pages to investigate the reasons which have brought about this decline of the sense of reverence. The fact itself is too evident to be in need of further proof. But it is very worth while to cultivate this sentiment. Reverence is not identical with deference. It is rather a peculiar attitude by which we become aware of the dignity of things and of human individuals.

It denotes a sad lack of respect if a man will go trampling down the flowers of a meadow regardless of their beauty. It is disrespectful to disturb the quiet of the woods by senseless howling. It is not less disrespectful to strew papers and empty cans on a beautiful spot on the shore of a lake. A man who uses a fine and costly blade to chop wood is behaving not only in a stupid but also in a disrespectful manner. So does one who tears out the leaves of a book to wrap up something.

Respect, in truth, means—in its fullest and most

literary sense—having a good look at a thing, becoming aware of its nature, using it according to its destination and handling it as it ought and deserves to be handled.

Respect is due to all things, whether they issued from God's creative will or are products of human industry and genius. The higher a thing ranks in the order of values, the greater is the respect due to it. Man being the highest creature within this tangible world, deserves the greatest amount of respect. There is a saying of Immanuel Kant, which without being absolutely true, contains a great truth: "All things," he said, "have a price; man alone has dignity."

This dignity human nature is invested with forbids that man be ever regarded as a mere instrument or tool or that he be considered as a mere element and factor. The true idea of human dignity became known to humanity only by Christianity. The notion of a human person being something altogether different from all other beings was hidden even to the greatest minds of the pagan world. When the sponsors of the French Revolution proclaimed the "rights of man" they did but repeat what Christianity had taught the world for eighteen centuries. But by detaching the "rights of man" from the religious background, where alone they find a support, these philosophers and politicians prepared the catastrophes of subsequent times.

We have to use things and we are entitled to do so. But we are not allowed to use our fellows. They are not in the world "for us"; they are there first for God, to do His will and to serve His ends, and secondly for themselves. They are not born to be used or misused by us, nor to be more or less pleasurable ornaments of our life, nor to be opportunities we may profit by or gain satisfaction from or just things we can take and leave at our pleasure.

Every man has, of course, certain duties towards his neighbors. We have those duties towards them, they have them towards us. The fact, however, of another neglecting the duties he has towards us is no excuse for our acting in the same way. His not behaving as he ought or even the sufferings his misbehavior brings to us do not dispense us from doing our duty. This is another of the fundamental truths man has to know if he wants to progress on the way of perfection and find an outlet for his troubles. The laws of morals are absolute laws, which amounts to saying that the obligation put on us is not influenced by any circumstances whatsoever. Many people, for instance, know that there is something amiss with their relations to others; they know even that they have to behave differently; they are even willing to change, but they expect others to change first. "I know," a man will say, "that I am treating my wife badly and I am quite disposed to change my behavior, provided that she first leaves doing this and begins doing that." The same words may be uttered, slightly modified, by a wife in regard to her husband or by a member of some social group in regard to his fellows.

They are, all of them, wrong. Their attitude is, of course, not unnatural, insofar as it is the result of primitive egoism; but it is surely contrary to morals and, therefore, to the laws of reality. The command to behave rightly is issued to every single individual; it is his personal duty to obey this command and there are no conditions whatever which may serve as an excuse. The very common habit of making the fulfillment of duties depend on conditions is but another trick played by an unruly will of self-assertion, or but the result of a very efficient though veiled craving for omnipotence. This behavior is, in fact, equivalent to making demands where there are no rights. Every man has to know that it is for him to begin, that he is not allowed to wait until another begins. By following this rule more successes may be realized than is generally believed, though it will take quite a time until this point is reached.

There is one truth more which has to be recognized ere man can start on the way of self-improvement. We all usually distinguish between more and less important things and deeds. In this we are quite right. But if we consider things from the point of view of moral progress, they assume a somewhat different aspect. There are, of course, greater and lesser wrongs; there are after all grave and light sins. But wrong is wrong, whether great or small. We can not, moreover, know for sure whether an action we deem to be but slightly wrong, may not, in the course of time, become the source of a very great evil. An old French legend tells of a good man whom the devil once came to tempt. The devil convinced this man, whose reason apparently was not very well developed, that he had to commit one bad deed; but he might, said the devil, choose among three propositions; he was free either to commit murder, or adultery, or to get drunk. The poor man thought he would choose, since choose he must, the lesser evil and promised that he would get drunk. So he did. Being drunk he ceded to the allurements of a woman; when he came home and his wife reproached him for having spent their money and having behaved scandalously, he got furious, gripped a knife and murdered her. Thus, the devil got him to commit all the three sins by inducing him to the least grave one.

This is, after all, but a legend, and a rather naïve one too. But it illustrates, and not unaptly either, a great truth. We ought to be careful whenever something appears to us as unimportant though as not altogether right. We ought rather to consider every moment of our life as an important one, as one which might become decisive for our whole future. We do not know what the effects of our words or acts may be.

This does not imply that we ought to be over-cautious or timid in our actions, or that we are not allowed to indulge in fun and pleasure. The knowledge of the possible importance of our actions should not become a means for shunning action altogether. But we have to know that we are taking certain risks in any action whatever. These risks can not be avoided, since omniscience and a knowledge of the future are denied to us. The more the central attitudes regulating our behavior are in accordance with the laws of reality, the lesser these risks will become.

2. *What to Do*

A man, having perused the foregoing chapters and wanting to get from them advice on how to deal with a particular difficulty, will probably feel that he has got nothing which could be of any help to him. He has indeed got nothing—as yet. The mere reading of the arguments exposed above, even acquiescing in them, is not enough. There are two kinds of assent; though both are assent, they are nevertheless very different by nature and by the effects they have on the human mind. We may see the truth of some statement without being really touched by it; our assent remains a thing merely of the intellect and it does not penetrate into the depths of our ego, not into the place where our will and our basic attitudes are rooted. It is as if there were, between our intelligence and the centre of our personality, something like a filter hindering certain things from sinking down into the deeper layers of our self. It needs quite a time and not a little effort to make the things we know to be true sink down into the core of our personality and become efficient there. Mere reading and the thought: "This is quite true," are not sufficient for causing a reforming or rebuilding of personality. It is only after these thoughts have become parts, as it were, of our very personality that they begin to influence our attitudes and the behavior resulting from these. Even if nothing more could be said on the topic of self-improvement than has been explained hitherto, a definite effect could be expected, not an immediate one indeed, but one developing slowly and often after quite a time.

All kinds of development need time; it is quite unreasonable to expect changes to set in all of a sudden. This may be the case in some exceptional situations, when the soil has been already prepared for a long time, though the person himself may be quite unaware of there going on within his being a slow but all-pervading revolution. But as a rule we observe slow and gradual evolution.

This slow process of transformation is very often not noticed at all by the subject in whose personality it is developing. A man may meditate on some moral truth and feel very convinced by it even when becoming acquainted with it the first time; he may notice no change whatever in the strength of his conviction, and nevertheless become gradually transformed. One morning he rises, so to say, another man, and he does not know what it was that brought about this change.

It is easy for a man who already knows clearly that he is making mistakes and that many of his troubles are of his making to let the ideas about the real reasons of his misfortunes sink into his mind. He will gladly accept an explanation, even if it is not to his credit, because he wants to get out of his unlucky state. It is quite another thing with a man who does not even suspect that he might be guilty of bringing about all his troubles, or at least a great deal of them, himself. It is indeed not easy to dislodge the ideas such a man has formed about the reasons of his difficulties. If he is told that he is an egoist, that he is greedy for success, mad with ambition, dominated by unruly pride, too much of a coward to strive earnestly for achievement and too much conceited to see his own faults and the limits of his nature, he will get furious or—if his manners do not allow for such a reaction—tell you that your words are pure nonsense. He knows, he will say, that he is anything but ambitious, that he is far from conceited; he knows for sure that it is not his fault if he does not get along with people, or is unpunctual, or given to a more or less immoral habit, or is not letting his religious life develop any farther. All this is due, such a man is sure to declare, to circumstances, to the wrong ideas others have of him, to his temperament, and—insofar as there can be the question of mistakes of his own —to factors which are beyond all control by himself. This is indeed the greatest handicap in all attempts to improve or to make another see how he could manage to lessen his difficulties—nobody is really willing to begin. They all, more or less, expect others to begin or circumstances to change, or something to turn up.

A man has to be, generally, in a pretty bad situation to think it even possible that he may be the cause of the unhappy state of things. But it can not be helped: the only way of helping oneself is to start with an absolute sincerity and a real good will. If the ideas explained before appear at first glance rather absurd, if they do all but appeal to our minds, we may at least consider them as a possible view; nobody can be expected to accept whole-heartedly and at once ideas which are so much at variance with all he used to think. But everyone may be expected to give some consideration even to ideas which seem to him altogether strange. These ideas are, after all, not nonsensical; they have been found to be true and to work in many, many cases;

they are propounded by men who have made the study of human nature their life's work. We have very often to devote some thought to ideas which at first appear to be rather phantastic or contrary to everything we believed. Such situations occur in science, for instance; to quote but one famous instance: the medieval scholars felt sure that the earth was standing still and the sun moving around it; but after the work of Copernicus had become known, the scientists had to abandon a statement they had believed to be absolutely true. (There were, however, some who did not feel this way. It is rather noteworthy that St. Thomas Aquinas held the geocentric theory but for a hypothesis of physics and conceded readily the possibility of another explanation. And during the fourteenth century there were some scholars who—long before the times of Copernicus —defended the heliocentric theory.) The fact that an idea is contrary to what was believed until now is no sufficient reason for refusing to look into the matter. A man who refuses absolutely to devote even a little thinking to unwonted ideas proves by this behavior that these very same ideas he rejects are true, since he shows himself to be conceited to the utmost, crediting himself with infallibility and incapable of an objective analysis of his own situation.

The first thing to do is, accordingly, to devote some thought to the interpretation of one's behavior. It is not necessary, it is even rather to be avoided, that one devotes too much time uninterruptedly to the research of the motivating forces at work in one's mind. By this one runs the danger of becoming easily discouraged and also of becoming unduly interested in oneself. The very first rule to be observed is, that the ordinary life, the daily work, the habitual occupations have not to suffer—unless some of the latter be of a kind to conflict with moral laws; a gambler, for instance, wanting to reform has not to continue gambling, telling himself that he will give it up when he has become sure of his true motives. But it were wrong, if a man would neglect his work or his family or even a harmless hobby and let self-analysis take up all his time. The descent into the depths of the self is, moreover, a tiring and a painful task; by forcing oneself too much one risks finding this task very soon too distasteful for going on with it. This self-analysis may, on the other hand, condition an interest in oneself very contrary to the real goal of these endeavors. As has been explained already before, we have to try to develop what can be called a disinterested interest, that is, to look at ourselves in the dispassionate and objective manner of a scientist. A person, however, not accustomed to analyze himself or his actions, may become quite enthralled by the discoveries he makes. There is a definite fascination in psychological analysis which may indeed become dangerous, because it distracts the mind from its real task and lets it become wrapped up with the study of mental things; in such a case this man will continue to observe very carefully whatever is going on in his mind, he will be interested in discovering, for instance, some egoistic motives where he did not imagine their presence, but he will content himself with just registering this fact without developing his discovery into a practical rule of action.

It is, therefore, advisable that the study of oneself and the search for the hidden motives of one's behavior be limited to a short time every day; ascetic theology recommends that one ought to devote some few minutes every evening to an examination of conscience, reviewing one's actions during the past day and taking notice of all faults committed. Something like this is also advisable in regard to the self-analysis spoken of here. But there is, of course, a great difference between the examination of conscience and the analysis of self; in the first case, man goes over his life during the last twenty-four hours to find out where he failed to do right, using his conscience and his knowledge of his motive as a guide; but self-analysis does not, at least in its initial stages, dispose of such a guide; it has as yet to discover the true motives especially in actions which seem all right from the subjective point of view. The difference is about the same as the one existing between confession and a talk with a medical psychologist.

Mental treatment has been considered repeatedly as an analogy to confession or even as something to replace confession. This idea is quite mistaken, for two reasons. First, it is obvious that no analysis and no discussion with even the cleverest psychologist can replace the sacramental factor of one's sins being forgiven. Second, it is to be noted that also the psychological structure of both these situations—in the confessional and in the office of the psychologist—are basically different. A man seeking advice from the psychologist because of some subjective trouble or some objective difficulty, may deplore these facts, but he need not repent them. His mental attitude is, accordingly, another from the very beginning; he wants to be helped, but not to be forgiven. But there is another element still more important. In confession the penitent accuses himself of what he knows to have been sinful or, at least, wrong; the man consulting the psychologist does not accuse himself; he complains of certain unpleasant experiences; the starting point is, to him, not the feeling of guilt, but the one of suffering. He does not confess this or that action as having been bad because of its having been prompted by wrong motives; he rather wants to be told how to behave so as not to get entangled in difficulties. Or to summarize this in a short formula: the penitent wants to become better, whereas the "patient" wants to become more efficient and more happy.

The difference pointed out in the last paragraph explains also, why the usual confessions prove so often inefficient in regard to improvement. Very wrong ways of behavior may be all right from the point of view of confession, because the penitent does not feel guilty at all; he even does not see any reason why he should mention this or that difficulty to his confessor, because he does not feel guilty and, accordingly, does not feel like discussing these things in the confessional. Take, for instance, a person who is incapable of decision; he does not commit a sin by not deciding; his chances of becoming guilty of a sinful action are even less than a normal person's; he does not discover any trace of sin in this behavior; why mention it at all? This person is, in a way, quite right; nor would the confessor feel it his duty to discuss such a feature of behavior; if a girl were to relate in the confessional, that she was unable to decide what kind of bathing suit she ought to buy, though it is already July, the confessor probably would feel that this does not regard him at all. But this fact of her not having a bathing suit, though she is going to leave for the beach within a few days, may be very important from the point of view of the psychologist and, accordingly, of self-analysis.

Since medical psychology has been mentioned, it will be as well to put in some few remarks on this subject. Many people who do not get on in life, especially, of course, when they believe, or have been told, that they are "nervous" turn today for help and advice to medical psychology or hope to get well by mental treatment. In this they are not wrong either. But one has to beware of the fact that there are different schools of medical psychology, which not only use different methods, but start from very different principles too.

Some of these schools profess theories which are in no way compatible with the principles of Christian ethics or Christian philosophy. It ought to be clear, from what has been said in the foregoing chapters, that mental treatment—in the full sense of the word—has always to deal with the total personality and, accordingly, with the general ideas of the individual. A treatment which is based on principles altogether alien to a person's faith will, therefore, be either inefficient or it will make havoc with, or even destroy faith. If a man feels that he ought to seek help from a medical psychologist, he will do well to take care that the one he turns to can be relied upon as to his philosophical and religious principles. Psychoanalysis as taught by the pupils of Freud is, for instance, absolutely incompatible with Catholic, even with all true Christian faith. A religious person, wanting to preserve his faith, has to inquire carefully what kind of psychology it is the psychologist follows, ere he entrust himself to his influence.

The first rule, then, to be observed refers to the time devoted to self-analysis; so does also the second. It states that we are not to expect quick results. The faults we want to overcome, the bad habits we want to get rid of, the mistakes we want to avoid, the difficulties we desire to escape are, usually, of long standing. It were not sensible to expect that things which have gone on for years and years will disappear within a few days or weeks or even months. Allusion has already been made to the fact that rebuilding a personality is a task which will last for years and which is, practically, never really completed. The things one has to deal with are, moreover, mostly hidden so carefully, rooted so deeply, so difficult to discover and so hard to uproot, that a long time indeed is needed for any noticeable success to be achieved. We know perfectly that we have to be patient when trying to influence another person; nothing is nearly so much in need of patience than education. The medical psychologist knows too that he can not transform a personality within a short time, and he will invariably tell his "patient" so. (There is a definite reason for putting this word between quotation marks; a man suffering from what is commonly called nervous trouble is indeed not a patient in the same sense as one suffering from some bodily disease. The differences, however, cannot be detailed here.) We are, however, rather impatient when our own self is implicated; whether it be the question of moral reform, or of changing our life, or of a physical trouble. We will tell another suffering from some disease and having to stay in bed that he has to be patient; but we become very impatient when we find ourselves in the very same situation. It is the same with everything related to ourselves. We know perfectly that education needs time; but we want self-education to proceed at a formidable rate.

For detecting the attitudes at work behind our undesirable habits or the mistakes we make it is better not to direct one's attention primarily just to the things which trouble us most. It is probable that there the unveiling will be more difficult then elsewhere, because these habits or troubles are just the screen behind which the unwished for qualities hide and the undecipherable mode by which they find expression. Man's nature being, as has been pointed out more than once, a unit, the very same attitudes must become visible also in other places. To get a true idea of our nature we can start with any action or feature of behavior whatever. By inquiring into the motivation of some behavior the person himself does not reckon as a nuisance or a bad habit, but which is felt in a somehow unpleasant manner by his fellows he may discover the reasons of other more important features of his behavior. It is especially worth while to consider little actions which are done without any particular intention and surely without any afterthought of aggression, even more or less involuntarily, and which offend or disturb others.

When one has made a mistake or behaved in a way one knows to be wrong, one feels naturally the desire to find some excuse. This desire arises not only when others criticize or resent our behavior, but also because man wants to silence the voice of his own conscience. An inquiry into the validity of these excuses will prove quite a good method for finding out something about one's hidden motives and about the tendencies governing one's behavior.

A man willing to make progress and to free himself of the undesirable qualities he may notice in his personality, desiring to diminish the amount of friction in his dealings with other people and with reality in general, will do well in remembering the main sources which are at the bottom of the difficulties of which human life is so full. Even if he does not, or not as yet, feel convinced of his being subjected to these dark forces, he will do well to think of such an explanation as a possible one.

The insinuation that one is an egoist, proud, ambitious in a wrong way, etc., is as a rule rejected very forcibly. It is quite a while before someone who has thus far given no consideration to this matter becomes even inclined to concede that these ideas may not be quite nonsensical. At first he will deny that there are any unknown motives or hidden attitudes at work in the human mind. After a certain time, if the facts are pointed out to him over and over again, or if he has devoted some reflection to the question and, perhaps, made some observations of his own, he may be inclined to concede the existence of these things—in other people. A rather long time will pass before he comes to see the working of the aforesaid forces in his own mind; even then he will only concede that such things exist and that he has found the statements he at first rejected to have been proven in this or that single case; but he will go on denying that the rôle played by these attitudes is as great as he had been told. It will be again quite a bit later when his eyes are opened to the truth about himself.

In trying to get some insight into his own personality, a man may use still another method. Lord Macaulay somewhere remarks that an author ought to strike out, in his manuscript, every sentence which pleases him particularly because, says he—and Macaulay knew something of writing and style—this sentence is sure to be bad. This advice may be applied also to the study of one's personality. It is quite useful to analyze such actions we feel particularly proud of; maybe this gratification of our pride or our vanity is not the effect just of the beauty or the goodness of our action; it may result as well from this action giving satisfaction to some of the more undesirable qualities of our self.

Every little knowledge about ourselves calls for corresponding endeavor for improvement. We have, happily, not to wait until we have reached a complete knowledge of our personality; thereon the necessary remarks have been made already in an earlier chapter. But the great question is how to proceed in bringing about or even for preparing this so very necessary improvement.

It has been pointed out more than once that a merely negative procedure does not promise much success. Even if we have become quite sure of pride or egoism playing an enormous rôle within ourselves, we are not able simply to suppress or to uproot them. It is much better to help the opposite tendencies to develop. Instead of trying to combat directly—in frontal attack, as it were—egoism and distrust against others and the tendency of finding fault with them and of criticizing them, we might, for instance, try to discover positive and even lovable features in each of them. No one is without some assets, so long as he is to be considered normal; it is different, of course, with the insane or idiots who, however, do not come in here. There is an old legend telling that once our Lord walking with His apostles passed a carrion lying at the side of the road, and that the apostles turned away full of disgust, remarking on the stench and the ugliness of the thing; but the Lord said: "Look at the beautiful white teeth." There may indeed be some beauty left even in a carrion and some good even in an utterly depraved individual. And we have not, as a rule, to do with carrions and depraved people. There is, strange to say, more willingness found in the average man for recognizing some little good in a criminal or some person of low morality, than in the people we meet in daily life. We are, in a way, more lenient against those we may, for some reason, condemn than with those we can not number with the black sheep.

It were not so bad, if we would use a little of the ingenuity we apply in excusing our own mistakes, to finding some excuse for the actions we disapprove in others.

To discover the good qualities in another person one has first to know him. It is a fact that we generally look at other people from a rather egoistical point of view; we ask ourselves whether this man may be of some help for our own ends, whether he will prove amusing, or interesting, whether we will profit somehow by having intercourse with him; but we do not ask what kind of a man he is—unless this question means again whether he is going to be of use—nor do we try to study him for his own sake. Mention has been made once before of the attitude of the scientist who studies in an objective manner the matter he is observing. This attitude is not the ideal one; but it is still many times better than that of criticism and distrust. If we cannot love our neighbor, we might at least become interested in him as a reality. Man is not less interesting than fishes or birds; but many people know quite a lot about fishes or buzzards and devote much time to finding out about them, while they do not care at all to find out about their fellows. Or they gather very precise information on broadcasting, screen technique, old Siamese idols and what not, but they neglect to become acquainted, even in a desultory manner, with the essentials of human nature. Knowledge of human nature is not to be got from books only; they are very instructive if they are of the right kind, but they do not supply all one has and ought to know. A man desiring to know about fishes will not content himself with reading books; he will go out fishing and observing the habits of fishes in rivers and lakes and in the sea. To become acquainted with human nature one has to observe man, to study his habits, to interpret his actions, to find out about his interests; there is no hope of learning how to deal with man unless one comes to know him really.

People who complain of being out of touch with their fellows, of not being able to fit into a company, and so on, are mostly not of a kind which induces others to receive them at first sight; they do not know what to talk about, they feel that they are boring others and are bored by them; but if they began to be really interested in people they would, after a time, discover how to get in touch. The proper study of mankind is man; this saying, old as it is, contains a great truth. There is in fact nothing within this world which can become as interesting, even as fascinating, as the study of man. It is indeed not so difficult to talk to another person when one knows what his main interests are.

Such an objective study of our neighbors is, however, more than just a method of becoming interested
in them; it helps also to develop real love of them, because the more the interest grows, the more the positive sides become visible. They are hidden, generally,
to our eyes, because of prejudice and, accordingly, a
one-sided and merely subjectivistic kind of knowledge.

Love, like every other virtue, is developed by training
or exercise. The emotional quality of love can not be
brought about by mere will. We can not command
our emotions and feelings. But love is not only an emotion; it is, and even very much so, an attitude of will.
Moral philosophy distinguishes an affective, that is an
emotional kind, and an effective kind of love. The
first is not produced at will; the second can be brought
about whenever a person is willing to behave in a loving way. We are not requested to feel like loving
everyone, but we have to act according to the commandments of love. By acting in this way, conscientiously and a long time, we not so seldom arrive at developing even the feeling of love.

As love for other people grows within personality the
love of oneself is gradually pushed into the background.
This way of dealing with an undue love of oneself
promises greater success than all attempts at suppressing
this egoistic inclination ever does.

It has been made clear before, that reason—if it has to
be called thus, even intelligence—is the very key which
opens the gate barring the way to perfection. Egoism
is best uprooted—as far as this is possible at all—by the
strengthening of the conviction that it is utterly nonsensical. Love of oneself makes the ego the centre of
the universe; the ego is credited with an enormous importance; good is what is good for the ego, bad only
what is unpleasant to it. Right is only what the ego
finds useful for its ends or fitting to its preconceived

ideas, and wrong is all that is of an opposite nature.
Reason can not but tell every sound mind that this position is unmistakably wrong. Reason can not but make
sure of the fact that a human individual is a very insignificant element within the whole of reality. Reason
teaches us that we depend to a very great extent on
other factors; our personality would not exist at all, if
there were not or had not been others to further its development; we ourselves would not exist at all, if others
had not taken care of us and we are still dependent on
others for continuing to exist; these very obvious
thoughts ought to convince us that we are not the ultimate aim of reality. Reason does even more. It shows,
if only we would trouble to use it in the right way,
that man's place in the great order of reality is not of
the kind to justify such an overrating of the ego.

The one great and truly important idea every man
has to become absolutely sure of is that there are laws,
independent of man's consent, ruling over reality and,
therefore, over man too, whether he be willing to recognize them or not, and that he has to bow to these laws
unless he wants to undermine his very own existence.
This point of view is familiar to the religious mind, or
it ought at least be familiar to it. But even a person
who does not believe in the articles of any faith or rejects religion altogether can not but see the truth of
this. Man is indeed serving his own ends better by submitting to the laws of reality than by revolting against
them and by trying to make his own small mind and
his own petty wishes the law of the universe. There is
a well-known text in the Scriptures implying this fact
by stating that man will save his life by losing it.

The attitude of egoism is not only wrong from the
point of view of morality, it is also stupid, because it
endangers in fact the existence of a person. To this
many will object, of course, that they know quite a few

people who are undoubtedly extreme egoists and who fare in spite of this or perhaps even because of this, very well. The egoist is believed to be successful, to achieve his ends because he is not hampered by moral scruples, to realize happiness because he is able to get what he wants. The old truism of the egoist never being happy because of his insatiability will not answer this objection, even though there is much truth in it. Another fact may carry more weight; unscrupulousness very often ends badly, because the laws of reality—and those of morality are real too—are not neglected with-out some punishment supervening. One need but read the papers to discover that many of those who attained wealth and influence and position by more or less dis-honest means meet punishment after all. The argu-ment that sins are punished hereafter may not impress the modern mind very much; even the religious mind of today has lost the sense of reality earlier times felt in regard to the future life. It is not to be pretended that a man addicted even to an excessive egoism feels troubled in his conscience, at least it is not the rule that he does, though there are many cases of this kind. He does not let his conscience trouble him, in truth, though his conscience is aware of the faults he made and makes. There is a way of escape, a compromise between the un-willingness of the ego to recognize its faults and the admonitions of conscience which never tires and never can be silenced completely; this escape and compromise is found in certain troubles known by the name of neurosis. Neurosis is, in fact, what one may call a moral disease; psychology speaks of neurosis as psycho-genic, meaning that its causes have to be sought for in mental facts; but it would be quite correct to speak of these troubles as "ethogenic," meaning that they spring from causes related to morality. It is, of course, un-known to what percentage the excessive egoists become a prey to neurotic disturbances; but it is well known that extreme egoism is the rule with all cases of neurosis coming under observation. From this one may conclude that egoism, at least its more pronounced forms, is not of a kind to guarantee a normal and happy life.

The idea of the laws governing the universe, regulating morally human actions, assuring socially the cooperation of the single individuals, has to be developed into a strong and unshakable conviction; it is the very basis of a normal life with the possible minimum of friction. All the theoretical arguments and practical advices on how to arrange one's life are in fact corollaries of this basic truth or derived from it. It is for philosophy and, in a still higher sense, for faith to give an answer to the question why these laws exist and whence they draw their power. The first thing to do is to recognize these laws as ruling over all things and over every individual as well. An attempt to revolt against these laws is as fruitless as stupid.

The very moment we become fully convinced of this fundamental truth we are led to the discovery that our nature is a rather limited one, that it is shut up within definite borders; wonderful though human nature is and astonishing though its achievements are, they are not allowed to pass beyond these borders. This is true of human nature in general, but also of every individual. Each of us has to recognize the limits set to him and his activity.

Not knowing about his limitation is one of the greatest dangers man may meet on the way to progress. By overrating his power he may bring on himself all kinds of misfortune. This is so evident that it need not be mentioned at all, if there were not a peculiar circumstance which intensifies this danger in one sense and lessens it in another. A man striving for goals he can never reach—be it that they are beyond his forces, be it that they are unapproachable by man in general—will meet failure; he may become broken, he may even meet death, but he need not suffer morally. Such a man is perhaps a truly tragic figure, but he may remain an absolutely upright personality. But a man of high-strung ambition who is not really striving for achievement, but only for success, and who, feeling incapable of realizing his ends, shelters behind excuses is not a tragic hero but—were it not for his subjective suffering—rather a comic person. There is also a definite element of immorality in this longing for things which are, by their nature and by the nature of man, beyond the grasp of human will; it is immorality because of the untruth it implies. Not recognizing truth which is visible to every eye willing to see is as contrary to truth as is telling lies.

The truth about man and his position within the total order of reality and the truth about the individual person's situation implies also the true idea of the order of values and, accordingly, of goals. It is generally assumed that, for the sake of pursuing the right goals with the desirable energy, an education or training of will is needed. But it has been shown that it is not really will which is in need of training, but rather purpose. Recognizing a goal as desirable in a general way, and truly striving after this goal, are two things. Not every idea of something being good or valuable is already a purpose. Nor is every purpose, or what mind believes to be one, already capable of moving will in its direction. These facts of psychology are very often neglected, even by certain psychologists. There are quite a few treatises on the training of the will, or on how to make the will stronger or on how to become energetic. These books are, generally, not worth very much. In fact, there is, so far as we know, only one which takes account of the results of psychological re-

search and of the true conditions determining voluntary acts; this book, a study of which will prove very
fruitful, is the small treatise entitled: *The Training of
the Will*, by Johann Lindworsky. The following remarks are largely indebted to Dr. Lindworsky's ideas.

The famous psychologist very strongly emphasizes
what has been pointed out here repeatedly: that we
ought rather to speak of good will than of a strong one.
The various ways proposed and followed to attain a
"training of will-power" are psychologically unsound.
It is true that in some cases certain methods may become
successful; athletics, training in sport, learning how to
endure hardships have been recommended as efficient
methods for acquiring a greater "strength of will."
There is, however, no guarantee that this method will
work out all right, since there are many people quite
capable of effort or endurance, for instance when training for some game or when camping, who nevertheless
fail to resist sensuous impulses, or to overcome their reluctance to systematic work, or their impatience when
dealing with their neighbors. These people learn to
make use of their will where and when it is worth their
while, that is, where and when they are sufficiently interested. But from such a success it does not follow at
all that this person will be able—that is, willing—to
exert his will on other occasions. The mental process is
even more complicated in some cases. A man complains
of his will being too weak for his doing what he ought
to do; he is told that going in for systematic training in
sport will help him in developing a greater strength of
will; being somewhat interested in sport and anxious to
secure some success he goes through his training conscientiously and indeed proves capable of quite remarkable achievements; but he does not develop a greater resistance against his impulses nor does he profit in regard to the overcoming of his bad habits. Having had

this experience he concludes that it is not his fault, if his will is not stronger; he has done what he had been told; he even achieved a notable progress; his failing in other fields can not, therefore, be attributed to unwillingness, it can not but be the effect of some deficiency of his organization for which he is not to be made responsible.

The idea of approaching the essential difficulties by a detour is useful in discovering the basic attitude, but it is much less so in attempting to uproot them. The fact just alluded to of a man acquiring "will-power" in one or, perhaps, in more than one field, but not in the one where it is most needed fits perfectly with the other, described before, of there being individuals who are incapable of enduring the boredom of work, though they are capable of enduring the hardships of, let us say, vagabondage. All these facts concur in demonstrating that there is no such thing as a general strength of will; there is, as Dr. Lindworsky so aptly remarks, but a good and a bad will. The problem is, therefore, not to strengthen the will, but to make it good.

There is, however, a kind of training which often proves useful; it ought not be called, strictly speaking, a training at all, or if it has to be called by this name, it is more a training of the sense of values than of the will. A man who, for instance, is rather unwilling to submit to rules or to take upon himself the unpleasant feelings accompanying work, might profit definitely by first learning to be punctual; instead of taking his meals just when he feels like, having lunch one day at noon and the next at half-past-two and then, just for a change, at eleven in the morning, he ought to make it a rule to have his meals every day at the same hour. This training may do a man good, if he enters it in the right spirit, that is, if he thinks it worth while to become used to regular hours, because this is right. But this training would probably not be very efficient if he did it because of himself. There is always this vicious circle threatening everyone who tries to improve: improvement means, in this matter, getting rid of oneself or, at least, detached from oneself; by trying to do so, a person becomes, on the other hand, interested in and attached to himself. The only way to break through this vicious circle is to strengthen in one's mind the idea, and to make it indeed the leading one, that improvement has to be sought for not because of one's happiness or efficiency or some other subjective aim, but because of its being objectively and intrinsically right.

The indirect way which has been recommended so often, proves after all to be not as efficient as it is said to be. It is preferable to seize the bull by the horns and to attack directly the faults and bad habits discovered in one's personality. But this attack has not to be—let it be said once more—a "frontal" attack and it has not to be limited to resistance against the things which ought to disappear. Developing an attitude opposed to the one which is felt to be wrong is a much surer way.

In trying to get rid of bad habits and to avoid habitual mistakes, it is of course most important to destroy the basic attitudes engendering the undesirable features of behavior. One will have to remember over and over again that it is pride or rebellion or cowardice or ambition which gives rise to so many unpleasant experiences. These basic attitudes, however, can be tackled and reformed only by getting hold of their manifestations. It is not possible to develop a general and, as it were, theoretical attitude, for instance, of humility; one has rather to learn how to behave humbly in definite and practical situations. For the sake of getting nearer to the realization of this purpose, one has to start with reforming just one of the bad habits or wrong

features of behavior. It is not possible to set about reforming all of them at the same time.

Another rule still seems to be rather important in
this respect. Many people believe that they have to
attack their bad habits each time these become manifest.
A man addicted to sudden anger will, for instance, pro-
pose to himself that he will not let himself get angry
any more. But he gets angry nevertheless, not only
once but rather regularly, whenever he has an opportunity for behaving in this way. His purpose of not
becoming angry any more is of no avail, because he gets
angry so quickly that he has no time left for thinking
of his purpose and of setting it to work. He feels,
therefore, discouraged rather soon and believes that
nothing can be done. It is more or less the same with
other things too. But this method is not the one which
ought to be applied. Nobody given to fits of anger can
be expected to get rid of them simply by wanting or
even by purposing to do so; it is one of the most characteristic features of these outbreaks of temperament
that they come on so very suddenly. A quite lengthy
preparation is necessary before one can hope to put the
brake on them. Another way of procedure has, therefore, to be chosen. We have—in the case of sudden
anger as well as in all the other instances of undesirable
behavior traits—to train for the right behavior during
the periods free from the manifestations of these traits.
St. Ignatius of Loyola remarks somewhere in his book
on the Spiritual Exercises, that neither the periods of
elation and exaggerated hopefulness—or of consolation,
as he calls them—nor the periods of dejection and despondency—of desolation—promise the greatest progress; it is the quiet time during which we may hope for
making real progress. Neither high nor low spirits
warrant the coolness of reason, the objectivity of judgment, or the determination and freedom of will which

are needed for forming a really efficient purpose. During this quiet time we have to build up the resolutions, which will, after having become sufficiently rooted in our personality, enable us to resist the outbreaks of temperament and the relapses into our bad habits. By reflecting on the reasons which made us angry, or despondent, or offended, or what not, the last time, and by making sure that these reasons did not really justify such a reaction, we become gradually able to keep a cooler head or to refrain from untimely emotional reactions.

A man will, however, gain by such meditations on the mistakes he made only if he is ready to use the utmost sincerity against himself, that is, if he puts away all thoughts of excusing himself. Many people when reflecting on their fits of anger, or of despondency, or on the last time they felt offended, will concede that the occasion as such did not justify their reaction. But they will have quite a series of excuses on hand; the person who made them angry had behaved in this way already so often that they could not help being angry; they would not have felt so offended if they had not had a similar experience just before; they would not have become depressed if they had not been unwell this day, etc. All these thoughts have to be discarded altogether; unless they are, no good will come from reflection.

To ponder on the reasons of behavior is more efficient than merely deciding to behave differently. The mere discovery of wrong reasons is, of course, not enough; they have to be replaced by the right one. It would be rather useless if a man were to concentrate only on what he does and on how he does it, without making sure of what he ought to do.

But many people know perfectly what they ought to do, or at least what is held to be the right thing by general opinion and the received code of morals, without this knowledge developing into motives. Mere reflection or meditation on the rights and the wrongs of the case is believed to be inefficient. It has even been alleged that the moving power of the higher values is very small when compared with the attraction the lower values exercise on the human mind. Those who make this statement have before their eyes apparently only the average situation man finds himself in. Before the true ideas of value, of the order ruling the universe, of the place man occupies within reality, have penetrated into the deeper layers of personality, the situation will be indeed more or less the one assumed in the said statement. But things become different after some consideration has been given to this matter. There is in man a mysterious reverence for truth; he can not shut his eyes completely so as to exclude from them altogether the light of truth. From the moment he gets even only so much as a glimpse of the truth, he feels attracted by it again and again; he need in fact do nothing but let the truth work in his interior according to its peculiar way. Not only in history, but in individual life too, will truth report the victory, though it may take quite a while until it does.

It ought to be impressed upon the minds of men that the pursuit of merely subjective aims, that the rebellion against reality and the attempt to make man the absolute master of the world are not only immoral, but very stupid too. Adult people very often behave as if they were still in the years of adolescence. Youth, having but an imperfect knowledge of reality, may be forgiven for taking exaggerated views of its own importance and for trying to realize aims which in truth are beyond the reach of man. But adults may be expected to behave in a more sensible manner. They close their eyes to truth, they try to see reality not as it is, but as they would like it to be. They do not see themselves as they are, but imagine themselves either to be supernormal beings or to be below the average.

Contradictory as these two attitudes appear to be, they have one very essential feature in common; they both place man outside of the average and credit him with an exceptional position.

It may very well be that one is—in some respect or another—above the average. But whether this is true or not, can be discovered only after the average station has been reached. Neglecting this fact is characteristic of the youthful mind. Youth has many pleasant features, and one understands well the desire of staying young as long as possible. But retaining the enthusiasm of youth, its fine quality of being easily inflamed, its optimism, and so on, does not amount to preserving the rest of the features of an adolescent mind too. An older person behaving as if he were still eighteen or twenty years old is not youthful; he is ridiculous. It is rather funny that most people try to "feel young again" not by trying to re-awaken within themselves the fine qualities of youth but rather its deficiencies and even stupidities. Few will try to feel young again by recalling to their minds the enthusiasm they used to feel when young, or by trying to get enthralled by a new topic as they were then, or by forgetting their habit of looking for drawbacks and by just drinking in the good and beautiful and lofty things—in which the world is not so poor after all—and to become rejuvenated; they rather prefer to turn to certain utterly accidental and superficial kinds of enjoyment. They seem to confuse youthfulness with foolishness.

It is quite true that a certain amount of youthfulness and the preservation of some of the fine qualities of youth could become very helpful and contribute quite a great deal to an improvement of individual life and of the general situation. But the main thing in this is not the repristination of the subjective features of youth, not of its way of feeling, etc., for the sake of feeling or else some subjective experience. The important thing is to recall the manner in which youth reacts to reality, to its good and bad sides. It is useless to become enthusiastic when this enthusiasm is not awakened by true and lofty values. The mistake made by so many people is that they are content to feel and do not trouble to ask what their feelings are about.

It can never sufficiently be enjoined that not feeling but the reasons of feeling, not the subjective state of mind but its correlated objective, not the strength of will but the goal will is aiming at, are of decisive importance. Nor can it ever become sufficiently emphasized that wishes and ideas do not count; only facts and actions have an influence on reality—for better or for worse.

To make clearer and more practical the remarks contained in the last pages, it will be well to show in a few concrete instances how they work out. For this some of the features mentioned in the previous chapters will serve best. No attempt at systematic grouping shall be made; the following remarks are nothing but aphoristic illustrations of things which have been discussed at length before. The examples which follow are—perhaps it is not unimportant to point this out—all taken from real observations. This fact may give them a greater amount of credibility and make them more alive than mere constructions ever could be; on the other hand these stories are individualized and they are, therefore, not to be applied just as they stand to another's individual case.

Since this question of the use of example has been touched upon, it will be as well to consider it a little, before describing the "cases." From studying the life and the behavior of other people one may, of course, learn many things. One may see what things to avoid and what things to do, but only in a rather vague and general manner. One discovers in another some quality and feels it to be rather unpleasant; there is perhaps something in one's own personality akin to this unpleasant feature, and the question arises, whether one's own behavior is not as great a nuisance to others as this person's is to ourselves. It is, without doubt, useful to give this idea some serious consideration. But then we become aware that there are, notwithstanding the definite similarity, still great differences; that we are not behaving in exactly the same way as does this person. There are, it is true, some ways of behavior which are very much alike even in very different personalities. It is a great mistake to believe that negative traits are in any way "original"; they are not; they are rather typical, and they become the more so when verging on the abnormal. The behavior of an insane person appears as "original" only to the uninitiated; the psychiatrist knows that it is more or less the same he has seen in so many other cases. Nor is "nervousness" anything which could remind one of originality; the nervous persons are—in what regards their abnormalities—very much like each other. It is only the normal and healthy personality which can be credited with "originality." There was a time when abnormality was considered, if not a criterion of genius, at least as something akin to it. The unlucky formula imagined by Lombroso—Genius and Insanity—has contributed much to creating this belief; but the thesis of Lombroso has proven to be quite mistaken, and the "craze" for abnormality has become markedly less. There are still, however, some people who try to show themselves different from and superior to others by cultivating a more or less abnormal behavior. But these people do not become, in fact, interesting; they are just nuisances and they are, as a rule, soon deserted and left to themselves; therefore, they have to try always to get new acquaintances and to leave them again before they are found out.

The observations we make on the wrong behavior of other people may help us in discovering the mistakes we make ourselves and also the reasons determining this behavior, since these reasons are, on the whole, always the same. But the observations on the right behavior of other people do not tell us more than what is right to do; they do not tell us how to do it. The higher the level of morality or perfection and, accordingly, of normality, the more individualized become the actions. This is a necessary consequence of the nature of individuality, as explained above. Individuality and, therefore, uniqueness of being become the more developed the higher the degree of perfection is. The more potentialities are converted into actualities, the more the characteristic features of an individual, that is, features this one being alone possesses, become manifest. It is therefore quite impossible for a man to become "a second St. Francis of Assisi" or "a second Napoleon." Every human being exists but once, and even more uniquely, as it were, the higher his degree of perfection is in any sense whatsoever. This fact constitutes a certain danger inherent to ideals.

Ideals ought to be what their name implies—ideas, but not persons. A person known from history—or, eventually, from fiction—may appear as the incarnation of a definite ideal and put the latter before our eyes; the importance of considering such a person is to be sought primarily in the conviction that this particular ideal can indeed be realized. Studying the lives of the saints we may be led to believe that sanctity is only something to be wished for, but never to be attained; we become, however, aware that sanctity may exist in living men of flesh and blood; by becoming acquainted with the lives of men who devoted themselves to the pursuit of an idea, to scientific research, to the spreading of faith, to works of charity, we gain the conviction that such a life may be realized, since it has been realized in these men. But each of us has, if it is given to him that he may realize some ideal or, at least, strive after its realization, to do this according to his own individuality.

Take the case of sanctity. Every age had its saints; but the ways of realizing a saintly life have been quite different at the different periods of history. Besides their determination of doing only God's will, there is but little likeness between a saintly anchorite of the first centuries of the Christian era, and St. Gregory the Great, or St. Francis of Assisi, or St. Ignatius of Loyola. Even saints belonging to the same religious Order differ widely in their personalities and their ways of religious life; the way of St. Teresa of Avila was not the one St. Thérèse de l'Enfant Jésus went, though they both were of the Carmelite Order. It is all right to practice some definite virtue as demonstrated by some saint, but there is no chance of ever really imitating such an ideal personality. Not because we may not, if such be God's will, become a saint too and even excel in the very same virtue, but because our individual person is absolutely unlike the one we admire.

The example of the saints and the problem of imitating them is only one very striking instance of a general rule. The right way of acting is doubtless traced out to us; but the manner in which we proceed along this way is different in every individual. It is only in the negative sides of their nature that men become so very much like each other. Instances of mistakes and of bad behavior allow, therefore, for more immediate application than do those of virtues and achievements. The idea of imitating exactly the life and the behavior of some ideal personality, e.g., a saint, sometimes becomes definitely dangerous and a serious handicap. A man wanting to be like his ideal can not but become aware rather soon that he is seeking a goal which can never be reached; he therefore becomes discouraged and gives up the pursuit of not only this, but of every ideal, because he has made this one the symbol of perfection.

To be even more concrete; the lives of the saints teach us the importance of sacrifice and self-abnegation. We may learn, by contemplating the achievements of the saints, that these virtues are within the reach of human nature, though their special development in each of these personalities is due, of course, not to human nature alone. Not even men great by nature as St. Augustine, or St. Bernard, or St. Thomas were, would have achieved the progress to perfection we admire in them without a peculiar help of God's grace. But it would be quite wrong for a man of business to lead the kind of life suited to a Cistercian monk of the twelfth century or to a bishop of the fifth. The attempt to copy exactly the life of the ideal ends generally in failure. There was a student of theology who had decided to become "a second St. Aloysius," and within a very short time too. He came soon to see that he would never reach his end, and being too vain to content himself with less, he gave up studying theology altogether, became an employee of the government and a very unhappy man for the rest of his life.

The idea of being entitled to realize a definite ideal is but one special manifestation of a general attitude which is wrong and dangerous. This attitude may be described as the feeling of having to get and not having got "one's due." It is indeed not "due" to a man that he realize just the one kind of life, of perfection, of religious state, etc., he imagines to be the best for him. Nor is it his "due" that he attain just the position in life he wants, or that he may use his faculties just in the way he desires. There are, in fact, no reasons why a man ought to be just what he wants; the one thing he has to do is to act in the best way in whatever situation he may be. It is an unhappy habit of most people to consider all they have not, instead of turning their eyes to the things they have. If they were sincere they would have to acknowledge that their not having more trouble is a rather wonderful thing. The chances of being unhappy, of meeting misfortunes, of suffering are so numerous that the average amount of trouble is less than one ought to expect. There is, of course, disease and penury and moral suffering and injustice; but many of the things men complain of are not as terrible as they believe them to be. Quite a large part of these things are, objectively taken, not so bad as those who have to suffer make them; many of the difficulties are, moreover, so bad only because people feel it to be an injustice that they have difficulties at all. If they did not feel that they are entitled to see all their wishes fulfilled and all their plans realized, they would suffer less. They are, very often, suffering so intensely only because they are not getting what "is due" them.

But is there anything that really is due to them? Is not Hamlet right in remarking: "Use every man after his desert, and who should 'scape whipping?" If we were treated by fate or Providence according to our merits we doubtless would fare worse than we do. Instead of complaining of our bad luck, we had better wonder at our not being treated worse than we are. This thought may prove a great help indeed, as is shown by the history of a girl of some thirty years. She was a teacher at a high-school and always felt that she did not get "her due," either from fate, or from her neighbors, or from the board of education; because she had always to insist on what she called her rights, she was easily offended, but she became offensive as easily, and was not, therefore, liked by the other teachers nor had she friends. She complained very much of being alone and of being badly treated by other people. Her loneliness and the feeling of being shut out made her rather nervous. She used to read a good deal, and by chance got hold one day of a book on the formation of character. Having learned from this book that a change of character could be brought about she contacted a psychologist. During the conversations this man had with the girl he pointed out to her that her basic attitude of wanting to get "her due" was quite wrong, that she did not and could not know what was due to her, and he quoted to her the aforesaid words of Hamlet. The girl being very intelligent and quite ready to accept advice, was very much struck by this remark and forthwith began to think it over. She soon saw that she was indeed overexacting and that she committed the very same faults for which she rebuked others. She devised a method for reminding herself of this by becoming accustomed to say by herself, every time she felt badly treated: "You don't deserve a better treatment; that's quite all right for you." In an astonishingly short time she developed a new attitude towards life and her neighbors; her religious life too profited very much, because she ceased to argue with God on behalf of her being "only His stepdaughter."

The development of such a personal maxim or motto is very often rather useful. St. Ignatius of Loyola recommends that a person about to become angry ought first, before answering, say silently a short prayer; the advice is good, because by this not only are we reminded of our religious background, but also because our mind is turned away from the immediate reason of our bad temperament. But it seems even more helpful to choose some thought or maybe prayer adapted to one's peculiar situation. A person given to fits of anger or of despondency or easily taking offence may, for instance, learn to think on such occasions: "It is not worth while," or: "This is nothing compared with a real cross," or something of a similar kind. That this method may become efficient is shown by the following "case."

A lawyer felt very much handicapped in his work by his becoming easily depressed; whenever things did not work out as he expected, he became quite despondent and lost all energy and presence of mind, a reaction which proved to be a great nuisance, especially in the courts. The main reason of this was, of course, his exceedingly high-strung ambition which made him incapable of meeting any failure with equanimity. He was one of those persons spoken of earlier who can not distinguish between defeat and failure. He adopted the habit of telling himself whenever such an opportunity for becoming depressed arose, that he was not entitled to expect his ideas to be realized. He condensed this thought in the one short sentence: "Remember that you are not omniscient." He too made great progress and learned to take things in a more normal way.

It has, however, to be pointed out, that one must not let this attitude develop in the sense of stoicism. This philosophy, of pagan origin, teaches an absolute indifference and equanimity; in this it is wrong, since there are things which have to stir up our emotions, things good and things bad. It were indeed wrong if we would become accustomed, just for the sake of avoiding unpleasant sensations, to consider everything as not worth while; it is definitely our duty to react on injustice— especially when suffered by our neighbor—or crime or, on the other hand, real heroism and goodness and beauty. The stoic attitude is not for the Christian mind; the "apathy" these philosophers used to preach amounts to killing all emotional reactions and, accordingly, to lessen the impetus towards the good and away from evil. From this stoicism arises often a wrong kind of tolerance which no longer distinguishes good and bad. We have to be tolerant towards people—do not judge, we are told, and you will not be judged—but not at all towards ideas or deeds. A bad deed is bad, even if we are inclined to find some excuses for the man who was guilty of this deed. The attitude of indifferentism, which is very common with the phlegmatic temperament, is not the one demanded by true morals. A person who endeavors to get rid of his overwrought sentimental reactions or his wrong outbreaks of temperament has to beware that he does not fall into the other extreme.

In many cases it may last a long time, until the person acquires the habit of remembering such a maxim as will help him in avoiding has habitual mistakes. He will go on making them and remember only afterwards what he ought to have remembered before. A training which has become established over a period of years is not broken within a few weeks; the person has been accustomed to react on every unpleasant sensation by a fit of anger or one of despondency, and this link between such an experience and the reaction thereon is not broken within a few weeks; the person has become ever, not without a certain influence. By associating the memory of the last instance of undesirable behavior with the memory of the disapproving afterthought, the habit becomes gradually and insensibly influenced. It is even more helpful, though it may not seem so at first, to devote some thought to one's wrong habits in a time when these are not actual at all.

A woman who suffered very much by her "sensitivity" and felt that everyone was treating her badly, had been told about the true nature of her character.

She understood, not willingly indeed, but she could not help seeing the truth, that she was very exacting and that she overrated her position and the honor she was entitled to very much. This idea did not help her at first; she went on being unhappy and feeling offended and disregarded and what not. But she adopted, after a time, the habit of analyzing the single instances after the emotional reaction had passed away. If it had been but slight, she was able to think things over the same evening; if it had been stronger she had to wait some days for cooling down. She found it also very useful to go over such instances which had occurred a longer time ago (such a person does not forget; they all remember every slight offence even had it been committed years ago). She turned her attention mostly on the instances in which she had been proved to be wrong; she had been offended by a friend not answering a letter, but this friend had been ill in a hospital; she had been shocked by someone alluding to certain things, but she became sure later that he knew nothing at all of these things. By analyzing her reactions in these cases she became more and more doubtful, whether she had been right at all. This thought led her on to a revision of her whole attitude which, by this, began to change slowly and even without this woman noticing the change. She became aware of it only, rather suddenly, when in a situation where previously she would have found herself very much offended and would have doubtless reacted accordingly, she remained rather cool and tried to find out what her interlocutor really meant to say.

This woman always knew, of course, that her behavior was not right; but this knowledge was of no avail until she became conscious of the reasons prompting this behavior.

Just one observation more may be added to make

plain the practical application of the ideas the foregoing chapters sought to convey. There was a boy of some twenty years who had come from a small town and had registered at the university. He had hoped to get in touch quickly with many of his fellows; but he was disappointed. The other students did not behave in an unfriendly manner, but they did not seem to care much for the newcomer. He soon felt quite alone and unhappy. He attributed his misfortune to the conceit of his comrades who, he said, apparently despised him because he came from the country and was, perhaps, somehow uncouth in his manners. He called them superficial and stupid because they did not try to find out what a fine fellow he really was. In this trouble he turned for advice to a psychologist whose lectures he attended. This man asked him, after having listened to his complaints: "Did you try to find out about your fellow-students?" The boy felt actually stunned by this question; he never had thought of his committing exactly the same fault for which he so bitterly reproached others. He objected, of course, after he had recovered from the shock, that he had no opportunity of getting in touch, not even so far that he could become acquainted with the personalities of his comrades. He was told to join a club which met every week to discuss matters of general interest: "You will not make friends immediately," said his mentor. "Content yourself with following the discussions, try to put in a word sometimes, better a modest question than a criticism; you will find an opportunity to be of use to someone, and so you will gradually become known and get in touch with others. First of all try to study your comrades and to observe their behavior among themselves, not in regard to yourself." The boy promised to do so; he joined this club, but for quite a time he did not feel that he had advanced towards his aim. He nevertheless, since he trusted his teacher, went on; one day after discussion, one of the students remarked that he would like to read a certain book and that he did not know where to get it. The boy took hold of this opportunity, owning this very book. "I could lend it to you," he said. "Oh, fine," replied the other, "have you read it?" And since he had, they became engaged in a lively discussion. This day marked a change in his relations with his comrades.

3. *Conclusion*

The subject with which this book had to deal is far from being exhausted. There are many things one could add and, surely, some readers would like to see added. But the book has not the presumption to pretend to be a kind of dictionary or an encyclopedia where one may find remarks on any matter whatever. An encyclopedia, e.g., on chemistry, has to contain all available information; it has to tell of the process of fabricating sulphuric acid as well as of the chemical nature of some dye. Even if it were possible to compile such an encyclopedia on human behavior—which is very doubtful —it would not have been what was intended here. The incompleteness of the description and explanation is, though forced on the writer by the necessary limitation of space and by his own restricted abilities, not something he would have liked to avoid. The basic idea being that all mistakes, or faults, or bad habits, and many of the difficulties of which human life is so full, arise from but few sources which are invariably the same, it seems really better to have the reader find out about the things which have not been mentioned here. A man who sincerely wants to improve and to get rid of certain habits will indeed profit more by discovering himself the reasons of his undesirable qualities than by being told exactly what these reasons are. The analyses given in the foregoing chapters ought to enable everyone to find out exactly what is the matter with him. If he conscientiously applies the methods used and the ideas explained here to his personal difficulties, he is sure to get at the bottom of things and to discover not only the reason why these things exist, but also the method of dealing with them.

The first and main intention of the writer is, to make people see themselves as they are and to show them that and how they may become different. Much would be gained already, if people came to recognize that many of their difficulties are of their own making, and if they would cease accusing others. A more severe view of our own nature and a more lenient one of the nature of our neighbors would doubtless contribute to make life run more smoothly. This leniency towards others is quite compatible with the strictest ideas of truth and right; leniency towards others is not permitted to degenerate into a washed out kind of "liberalism," which indeed is but a more pleasant name for an utterly immoral indifferentism.

This, then, is the second and accessory aim this book is pursuing. It wants to make clear that a happy life, that getting along with one's neighbors, doing good work, making progress in perfection, attaining a higher level of religious state, depend very much on our recognizing the basic truths about man and reality. It has been remarked in the preface to this book that one need not be a philosopher for becoming better. But being a philosopher in the strict sense of the term and having a philosophy are two rather different things. Each man indeed has some philosophy of his own, whether he is conscious of it or not; and he lives according to this philosophy or "world view." It is one of man's foremost duties to find out about his basic ideas on himself and on the world in general, and to correct these ideas according to the invariable and inviolable standards of truth.

But the truth about man is that he holds a very ambiguous position within reality. He has been "crowned with honor and glory and set over the works of Thy hands"; but this crown has been given to him and he did not put it on his head himself; the works over which man is set, are not his own works. There are eternal laws ruling over the universe and over man too, who is but one element within this universe. Recognizing these laws is not yet humility, but it may be the first step towards this virtue; nor is a full consciousness of these laws equivalent to true piety, but it may be a beginning. "Piety," it is written, "is good for everything."

INDEX

Book Order Form

Please send me the following books:

Quantity	Title	Price per book	Total
	Self Improvement	$ 19.95	

Shipping/Handling charges: $2.95 for the first book, 75 cents for each additional book. Please allow 3 to 4 weeks for delivery	Postage/ Handling	
	TOTAL	

Enclosed is my [ ] check or [ ] money order (in U.S. Dollars) made payable to **Roman Catholic Books**.

[ ] Yes, please place me on your mailing list to receive your full catalog of books.

Please print:

Name: _____

Address: _____

City/State/Zip: _____

Telephone #: _____

Mail your order to:

Roman Catholic Books
A Division of Catholic Media Apostolate
Post Office Box 2286, Fort Collins, CO 80522